GLIMPSE AFTER GLIMPSE

GLIMPSE AFTER GLIMPSE

Daily Reflections on Living and Dying

Sogyal Rinpoche

With Original Calligraphy by the Author

HarperSanFrancisco
A Division of HarperCollinsPublishers

FIRST EDITION

Library of Congress Cataloging-in-Publication Data

Sogyal, Rinpoche.
Glimpse after glimpse : daily reflections on living and dying / Sogyal Rinpoche. Original calligraphy by the author. — 1st ed.
p. cm.
ISBN 0–06–251126–2
1. Buddhist devotional calendars. 2. Rdzogs-chen (Rñin-ma-pa) I. Title.
BQ5580.S65   1995
294.3'443—dc20   94-41924

95 96 97 98 99 ❖ HAD 10 9 8 7 6 5 4 3 2 1

I would like to dedicate this book to
Guru Rinpoche, the buddha of our time.

O Guru Rinpoche, Precious One,
You are the embodiment of
The compassion and blessings of all the buddhas,
The only protector of beings.
My body, my possessions, my heart and soul
Without hesitation, I surrender to you!
From now until I attain enlightenment,
In happiness or in sorrow, in circumstances good or
 bad, in situations high or low:
I rely on you completely, O Padmasambhava, you
 who know me:
Inspire me, guide me, make me one with you!

One glimpse is

not enough !

January 1

According to the wisdom of Buddha, we can actually use our lives to prepare for death. We do not have to wait for the painful death of someone close to us or the shock of terminal illness to force us to look at our lives. Nor are we condemned to go out empty-handed at death to meet the unknown. We can begin, here and now, to find meaning in our lives. We can make of every moment an opportunity to change and to prepare—wholeheartedly, precisely, and with peace of mind—for death and eternity.

January 2

Learning to meditate is the greatest gift you can give yourself in this life. For it is only through meditation that you can undertake the journey to discover your true nature, and so find the stability and confidence you will need to live, and die, well.

Meditation is the road to enlightenment.

January 3

When I teach meditation, I often begin by saying: "Bring your mind home. And release. And relax."

To *bring your mind home* means to bring the mind into the state of Calm Abiding through the practice of mindfulness. In its deepest sense, to bring your mind home is to turn your mind inward and rest in the nature of mind. This itself is the highest meditation.

To *release* means to release the mind from its prison of grasping, since you recognize that all pain and fear and distress arise from the craving of the grasping mind. On a deeper level, the realization and confidence that arise from your growing understanding of the nature of mind inspire the profound and natural generosity that enables you to release all grasping from your heart, letting it free itself to melt away in the inspiration of meditation.

To *relax* means to be spacious and to relax the mind of its tensions. More deeply, you relax into the true nature of your mind, the state of Rigpa. It is like pouring a handful of sand onto a flat surface, and each grain settles of its own accord. This is how you relax into your true nature, letting all thoughts and emotions naturally subside and dissolve into the state of the nature of mind.

January 4

How many of us are swept away by what I have come to call an "active laziness"? Naturally there are different species of laziness: Eastern and Western. The Eastern style consists of hanging out all day in the sun, doing nothing, avoiding any kind of work or useful activity, drinking cups of tea and gossiping with friends.

Western laziness is quite different. It consists of cramming our lives with compulsive activity, so that there is no time left to confront the real issues.

If we look into our lives, we will see clearly how many unimportant tasks, so-called "responsibilities" accumulate to fill them up. One master compares them to "housekeeping in a dream." We tell ourselves we want to spend time on the important things of life, but there never *is* any time.

Helpless, we watch our days fill up with telephone calls and petty projects, with so many responsibilities—or should we call them "irresponsibilities"?

Loss and bereavement can remind you sharply of what can happen when in life you do not show your love and appreciation, or ask for forgiveness, and so make you far more sensitive to your loved ones.

Elisabeth Kübler-Ross said: "What I try to teach people is to live in such a way that you say those things while the other person can still hear it." And Raymond Moody, after his life's work in near-death research, wrote: "I have begun to realize how near to death we all are in our daily lives. More than ever now I am very careful to let each person I love know how I feel."

January 6

One powerful way to evoke compassion is to think of others as exactly the same as you. "After all," the Dalai Lama explains, "all human beings are the same—made of human flesh, bones, and blood. We all want happiness and want to avoid suffering. Further, we have an equal right to be happy. In other words, it is important to realize our sameness as human beings."

January 7

Despite all our chatter about being practical, to be practical in the West means to be ignorantly, and often selfishly, short-sighted. Our myopic focus on *this* life, and this life only, is the great deception, the source of the modern world's bleak and destructive materialism. No one talks about death and no one talks about the afterlife, because people are made to believe that such talk will only thwart our so-called progress in the world.

If our deepest desire is truly to live and go on living, why do we blindly insist that death is the end? Why not at least try to explore the possibility that there may be a life after? Why, if we are as pragmatic as we claim, don't we begin to ask ourselves seriously: Where does our *real* future lie? After all, very few of us live longer than a hundred years. And after that there stretches the whole of eternity, unaccounted for. . . .

January 8

From the Tibetan Buddhist point of view, we can divide our entire existence into four continuously inter-linked realities:

1. life; 2. dying and death; 3. after death; and 4. rebirth.

These are known as the four bardos:

1 the natural bardo of this life,
2 the painful bardo of dying,
3 the luminous bardo of dharmata, and
4 the karmic bardo of becoming.

The bardos are particularly powerful opportunities for liberation because there are, the teachings show us, certain moments that are much more powerful than others and much more charged with potential, when whatever you do has a crucial and far-reaching effect.

I think of a bardo as being like a moment when you step toward the edge of a precipice; such a moment, for example, is when a master introduces a disciple to the essential, original, and innermost nature of his or her mind. The greatest and most charged of these moments, however, is the moment of death.

January 9

Nothing has any *inherent* existence of its own when you really look at it, and this absence of independent existence is what we call "emptiness." Think of a tree. When you think of a tree, you tend to think of a distinctly defined object; and on a certain level it is. But when you look more closely at the tree, you will see that ultimately it has no independent existence.

When you contemplate it, you will find that it dissolves into an extremely subtle net of relationships that stretches across the universe. The rain that falls on its leaves, the wind that sways it, the soil that nourishes and sustains it, all the seasons and the weather, moonlight and starlight and sunlight—all form part of this tree.

As you begin to think more and more about the tree, you will discover that everything in the universe helps to make the tree what it is; that it cannot at any moment be isolated from anything else; and that at every moment its nature is subtly changing. This is what we mean when we say things are empty, that they have no independent existence.

January 10

When a much larger number of people know the nature of their minds, they'll know also the glorious nature of the world they are in, and will struggle urgently and bravely to preserve it. It's interesting that the Tibetan word for "Buddhist" is *nangpa*. It means "inside-er": someone who seeks the truth not outside but within the nature of his or her mind. All the teachings and training in Buddhism are aimed at that one single point: to look into the nature of mind, and so free us from the fear of death and help us realize the truth of life.

January 11

The Buddhist meditation masters know how flexible and workable the mind is. If we train it, anything is possible. In fact, we are already perfectly trained by and for samsara, trained to get jealous, trained to grasp, trained to be anxious and sad and desperate and greedy, trained to react angrily to whatever provokes us. In fact, we are trained to such an extent that these negative emotions rise spontaneously, without our even trying to generate them.

So everything is a question of training and the power of habit. Devote the mind to confusion and we know only too well, if we're honest, that it will become a dark master of confusion, adept in its addictions, subtle and perversely supple in its slaveries. Devote it in meditation to the task of freeing itself from illusion, and we will find that with time, patience, discipline, and the right training, the mind will begin to unknot itself and know its essential bliss and clarity.

January 12

One of the chief reasons we have so much anguish and difficulty in facing death is that we ignore the truth of impermanence.

In our minds, changes always equal loss and suffering. And if they come, we try to anesthetize ourselves as far as possible. We assume, stubbornly and unquestioningly, that permanence provides security and impermanence does not. But in fact impermanence is like some of the people we meet in life—difficult and disturbing at first, but on deeper acquaintance far friendlier and less unnerving than we could have imagined.

January 13

Human beings spend all their lives preparing, preparing, preparing. . . . Only to meet the next life unprepared.

DRAKPA GYALTSEN

What is the nature of mind like? Imagine a sky, empty, spacious, and pure from the beginning; its *essence* is like this. Imagine a sun, luminous, clear, unobstructed, and spontaneously present; its *nature* is like this. Imagine that sun shining out impartially on us and all things, penetrating all directions; its *energy*, which is the manifestation of compassion, is like this: Nothing can obstruct it, and it pervades everywhere.

January 15

An effortless compassion can arise for all beings
who have not realized their true nature. So limitless is
it that if tears could express it, you would cry without
end. Not only compassion, but tremendous skillful
means can be born when you realize the nature of
mind. Also you are naturally liberated from all suffering and fear, such as the fear of birth, death and the intermediate state. Then if you were to speak of the joy
and bliss that arise from this realization, it is said by
the buddhas that if you were to gather all the glory, en-
joyment, pleasure and happiness of the world and put
it all together, it would not approach one tiny fraction
of the bliss that you experience upon realizing the nature of mind.

NYOSHUH KHEN RINPOCHE

January 16

How hard it can be to turn our attention within! How easily we allow our old habits and set patterns to dominate us! Even though they bring us suffering, we accept them with almost fatalistic resignation, for we are so used to giving in to them. *We may idealize freedom, but when it comes to our habits, we are completely enslaved.*

Still, reflection can slowly bring us wisdom. We may, of course, fall back into fixed repetitive patterns again and again, but slowly we *can* emerge from them and change.

January 17

In Tibetan, the word for "body" is *lü,* which means "something you leave behind," like baggage. Each time we say *lü,* it reminds us that we are only travelers, taking temporary refuge in this life and this body. In Tibet, people did not distract themselves by spending all their time trying to make their external circumstances more comfortable. They were satisfied if they had enough to eat, clothes on their backs, and a roof over their heads.

Going on, as we do, obsessively trying to improve our conditions, can become an end in itself, and a pointless distraction. Would people in their right mind think of fastidiously redecorating their hotel room every time they checked in to one?

January 18

Karma is not fatalistic or predetermined. Karma means *our* ability to create and to change. It is creative because we *can* determine how and why we act. We *can* change. The future is in our hands, and in the hands of our heart.

Buddha said:

> *Karma creates all, like an artist,*
> *Karma composes, like a dancer.*

January 19

In Tibetan we call the essential nature of mind
Rigpa—primordial, pure, pristine awareness that is at
once intelligent, cognizant, radiant, and always awake.
This nature of mind, its innermost essence, is absolutely and always untouched by change or death. At
present it is hidden within our own mind, our *sem,* enveloped and obscured by the mental scurry of our
thoughts and emotions. Just as clouds can be shifted by
a strong gust of wind to reveal the shining sun and
wide-open sky, so, under certain circumstances, some
inspiration may uncover for us glimpses of this nature
of mind. These glimpses have many depths and degrees, but each of them will bring some light of understanding, meaning and freedom.

This is because the nature of mind is the very root
itself of understanding.

January 20

Our minds can be wonderful, but at the same time they can be our very worst enemy. They give us so much trouble. Sometimes I wish the mind were like a set of dentures, which we could take out and leave on our bedside table overnight. At least we would get a break from its tiring and tiresome escapades.

We are so at the mercy of our minds that even when we find that the spiritual teachings strike a chord inside us, and move us more than anything we have ever experienced, still we hold back, because of some deep-seated and inexplicable suspicion.

Somewhere along the line, though, we have to stop mistrusting. We have to let go of the suspicion and doubt, which are supposed to protect us but never work, and only end up hurting us even more than what they are supposed to defend us from.

January 21

One method of meditation that many people find useful is to rest the mind lightly on an object. You can use an object of natural beauty that invokes a special feeling of inspiration for you, such as a flower or a crystal. But something that embodies the truth, such as an image of Buddha, or Christ, or particularly your master, is even *more* powerful.

Your master is your living link with the truth, and because of your personal connection to your master, just *seeing* his or her face connects you to the inspiration and truth of your own nature.

January 22

Imagine a person who suddenly wakes up in the hospital after an automobile accident to find that she is suffering from total amnesia. Outwardly, everything is intact: She has the same face and form, her senses and her mind are there, but she doesn't have any idea or any trace of a memory of who she really is.

In exactly the same way, we cannot remember our true identity, our original nature. Frantically, and in real dread, we cast around and improvise another identity, one we clutch with all the desperation of someone falling continuously into an abyss. This false and ignorantly assumed identity is "ego."

It cannot be stressed too often that it is *the truth of the teaching* that is all-important, and never the personality of the teacher. This is why Buddha reminded us in the *Four Reliances:*

> *Rely on the message of the teacher, not on his personality;*
> *Rely on the meaning, not just on the words;*
> *Rely on the real meaning, not on the provisional one;*
> *Rely on your wisdom mind, not on your ordinary, judgmental mind.*

It is important to remember that the true teacher *is* the spokesman of the truth: its compassionate "wisdom display." All the buddhas, masters, and prophets are the emanations of this truth, appearing in countless skillful, compassionate guises in order to guide us, through their teachings, back to our true nature.

At first, more important than finding the teacher is finding and following the truth of the teaching, for it is through making a connection with the truth of the teaching that you will discover your living connection with a master.

January 24

In my tradition we revere the masters for being even kinder than the buddhas themselves. Although the compassion and power of the buddhas are always present, our obscurations prevent us from meeting the buddhas face to face. But we *can* meet the masters; they are here, living, breathing, speaking, and acting before us to show us, in all the ways possible, the path of the buddhas: the way to liberation.

For me, my masters have been the embodiment of living truth, undeniable signs that enlightenment is possible in a body, in this life, in this world, even here and even now, the supreme inspirations in my practice, in my work, in my life, and in my journey toward liberation. My masters are for me the embodiments of my sacred commitment to keep enlightenment foremost in my mind until I actually achieve it. I know enough to know that only when I reach enlightenment will I have a complete understanding of who they really are and of their infinite generosity, love, and wisdom.

January 25

The compassionate wish to attain enlightenment for the benefit of all others is called Bodhicitta in Sanskrit; *bodhi* refers to our enlightened essence, and *citta* means "heart." So we could translate it as "the heart of our enlightened mind." To awaken and develop the heart of the enlightened mind is to ripen steadily the seed of our buddha nature, that seed that, in the end, when our practice of compassion has become perfect and all-embracing, will flower majestically into buddhahood. Bodhicitta, then, is the spring and source and root of the entire spiritual path. This is why in our tradition we pray with such urgency:

> *Those who haven't yet given birth to precious*
> *Bodhicitta,*
> *May they give birth,*
> *Those who have given birth,*
> *May their Bodhicitta not lessen but*
> *Increase further and further.*

January 26

The purpose of reflection on death is to make a real change in the depths of our hearts. Often this will require a period of retreat and deep contemplation, because only that can truly open our eyes to what we are doing with our lives.

Contemplation on death will bring you a deepening sense of what we call "renunciation," in Tibetan *ngé jung*. *Ngé* means "actually" or "definitely," and *jung* to "come out," "emerge" or "be born." The fruit of frequent and deep reflection on death will be that you will find yourself emerging, often with a sense of disgust, from your habitual patterns. You will find yourself increasingly ready to let go of them, and in the end you will be able to free yourself from them as smoothly, the masters say, "as drawing a hair from a slab of butter."

January 27

The Dzogchen Tantras, the ancient teachings from which the bardo instructions come, speak of a mythical bird, the *garuda*, which is born fully grown. This image symbolizes our primordial nature, which is already completely perfect. The garuda chick has all its wing feathers fully developed inside the egg, but it cannot fly before it hatches. Only at the moment when the shell cracks open can it burst out and soar up into the sky. Similarly, the masters tell us, the qualities of buddha-hood are veiled by the body, and as soon as the body is discarded, they will be radiantly displayed.

January 28

The still revolutionary insight of Buddhism is that *life and death are in the mind, and nowhere else*. Mind is revealed as the universal basis of experience—the creator of happiness and the creator of suffering, the creator of what we call life and what we call death.

January 29

Dudjom Rinpoche was driving through France with his wife, admiring the countryside as they went along. They passed a long cemetery that had been freshly painted and decorated with flowers. Dudjom Rinpoche's wife said: "Rinpoche, look how everything in the West is so neat and clean. Even the places where they keep corpses are spotless. In the East not even the houses that people live in are anything like as clean as this."

"Ah, yes," he replied, "that's true; this is such a civilized country. They have such marvelous houses for dead corpses. But haven't you noticed? They have such wonderful houses for the living corpses too."

January 30

If you are sitting, and your mind is not wholly in tune with your body—if you are, for instance, anxious or preoccupied with something—your body will experience physical discomfort, and difficulties will arise more easily. Whereas if your mind is in a calm, inspired state, it will influence your whole posture, and you can sit much more naturally and effortlessly. So it is very important to unite the posture of your body and the confidence that arises from your realization of the nature of your mind.

January 31

What is the View? It is nothing less than *seeing* the actual state of things as they are; it is *knowing* that the true nature of mind is the true nature of everything; and it is *realizing* that the true nature of mind is the absolute truth.

Dudjom Rinpoche says: "The View is the comprehension of the naked awareness, within which everything is contained: sensory perception and phenomenal existence, samsara and nirvana. This awareness has two aspects: 'emptiness' as the absolute, and 'appearances' or 'perception' as the relative."

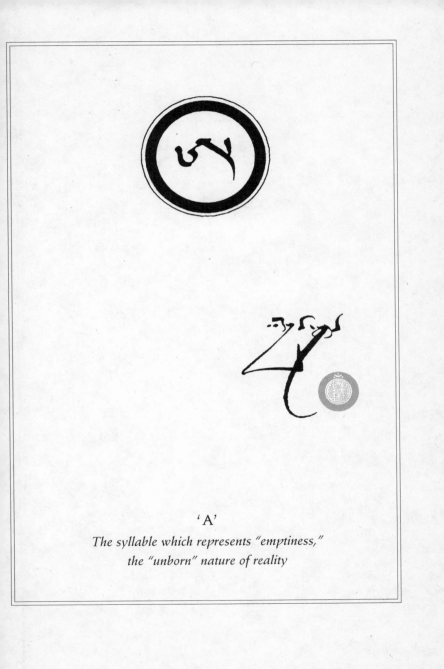

'A'

The syllable which represents "emptiness,"
the "unborn" nature of reality

February 1

More than twenty-five hundred years ago, a man who had been searching for the truth for many, many lifetimes came to a quiet place in northern India and sat down under a tree. He continued to sit under the tree, with immense resolve, and vowed not to get up until he had found the truth.

At dusk, it is said, he conquered all the dark forces of delusion; and early the next morning, as the planet Venus broke in the dawn sky, the man was rewarded for his age-long patience, discipline, and flawless concentration by achieving the final goal of human existence: enlightenment.

At that sacred moment, the earth itself shuddered, as if "drunk with bliss," and, as the scriptures tell us: "No one anywhere was angry, ill or sad; no one did evil, none was proud; the world became quite quiet, as though it had reached full perfection." This man became known as Buddha.

February 2

Grasping is the source of all our problems. Since impermanence to us spells anguish, we grasp on to things desperately, even though all things change. We are terrified of letting go, terrified, in fact, of living at all, *since learning to live is learning to let go*. And this is the tragedy and the irony of our struggle to hold on: Not only is it impossible, but it brings us the very pain we are seeking to avoid.

The intention behind grasping may not in itself be bad; there's nothing wrong with the desire to be happy, but what we try to grasp on to is by nature ungraspable.

The Tibetans say that you cannot wash the same dirty hand twice in the same running river, and "no matter how much you squeeze a handful of sand, you will never get oil out of it."

February 3

A wave in the sea, seen in one way, seems to have a distinct identity, an end and a beginning, a birth and a death. Seen in another way, the wave itself doesn't really exist but is just the behavior of water, "empty" of any separate identity but "full" of water. So when you really think about the wave, you come to realize that it is something that has been made temporarily possible by wind and water, and is dependent on a set of constantly changing circumstances. You also realize that every wave is related to every other wave.

February 4

Whatever we have done with our lives makes us what we are when we die. And everything, absolutely everything, counts.

February 5

What is meditation in Dzogchen? It is simply resting, undistracted, in the View, once it has been introduced.

Dudjom Rinpoche describes it: "Meditation consists of being attentive to such a state of Rigpa, free from all mental constructions, whilst remaining fully relaxed, without any distraction or grasping. For it is said that 'meditation is not striving, but naturally becoming assimilated into it.'"

February 6

The cells of our body are dying, the neurons in our brain are decaying, even the expressions on our face are always changing, depending on our mood. What we call our basic character is only a "mindstream," nothing more. Today we feel good because things are going well; tomorrow we feel the opposite. Where did that good feeling go?

What could be more unpredictable than our thoughts and emotions: Do you have any idea what you are going to think or feel next? The mind, in fact, is as empty, as impermanent, and as transient as a dream. Look at a thought: It comes, it stays, and it goes. The past is past, the future not yet risen, and even the present thought, as we experience it, becomes the past.

The only thing we really have is nowness, is now.

THE ESSENTIAL NATURE OF MIND

No words can describe it
No example can point to it
Samsara does not make it worse
Nirvana does not make it better
It has never been born
It has never ceased
It has never been liberated
It has never been deluded
It has never existed
It has never been nonexistent
It has no limits at all
It does not fall into any kind of category.

DUDJOM RINPOCHE

February 8

A human being is part of a whole, called by us the 'Universe,' a part limited in time and space. He experiences himself, his thoughts and feelings, as something separated from the rest—a kind of optical delusion of his consciousness. This delusion is a kind of prison for us, restricting us to our personal desires and to affection for a few persons nearest us. Our task must be to free ourselves from this prison by widening our circles of compassion to embrace all living creatures and the whole of nature in its beauty.

ALBERT EINSTEIN

February 9

Doubts demand from us a real skillfulness in dealing with them, and I notice how few people have any idea how to pursue doubts or to use them. It seems ironic that in a civilization that so worships the power of deflation and doubt, hardly anyone has the courage to deflate the claims of doubt itself—to do as one Hindu master said: turn the dogs of doubt on doubt itself, to unmask cynicism, and to uncover what fear, despair, hopelessness, and tired conditioning it springs from. Then doubt would no longer be an obstacle, but a door to realization, and whenever doubt appeared in the mind, a seeker would welcome it as a means of going deeper into the truth.

February 10

Ego is the absence of true knowledge of who we really are, together with its result: a doomed clutching on, at all costs, to a cobbled together and makeshift image of ourselves, an inevitably chameleon charlatan self that keeps changing, and has to, to keep alive the fiction of its existence.

In Tibetan, ego is called *dakdzin,* which means "grasping to a self." Ego is then defined as incessant movements of grasping at a delusory notion of "I" and "mine," self and other, and all the concepts, ideas, desires, and activities that will sustain that false construction.

Such grasping is futile from the start and condemned to frustration, for there is no basis or truth in it, and what we are grasping at is by its very nature ungraspable. The fact that we need to grasp at all and to go on grasping shows that in the depths of our being we know that the self doesn't inherently exist. From this secret, unnerving knowledge spring all our fundamental insecurities and fears.

February 11

Your compassion can have perhaps three essential benefits for a dying person: First, because it is opening your heart, you will find it easier to show the dying person the unconditional love he or she needs so much.

On a deeper, spiritual level, I have seen again and again how, if you can embody compassion and act out of the heart of compassion, you will create an atmosphere in which the other person can be inspired to imagine the spiritual dimension or even take up spiritual practice.

On the deepest level of all, if you constantly practice compassion for the dying person, and in turn inspire him or her to do the same, you might heal the person not only spiritually but perhaps even physically. And you will discover for yourself, with wonder, what all the spiritual masters know: that *the power of compassion has no bounds.*

February 12

A Zen master had a faithful but very naive student
who regarded him as a living buddha. One day the
master accidentally sat down on a needle. He screamed
"Ouch" and jumped into the air. The student instantly
lost all his faith and left, saying how disappointed he
was to find that his master was not fully enlightened.
Otherwise, he thought, how could he jump up and
scream out loud like that? The master was sad when
he realized his student had left, and said: "Alas, poor
man! If only he had known that in reality neither I, nor
the needle, nor the 'ouch' really existed."

February 13

Remember the example of an old cow:
She's content to sleep in a barn.
You have to eat, sleep and shit—
That's unavoidable—anything
Beyond that is none of your business.
Do what you have to do
And keep yourself to yourself.

PATRUL RINPOCHE
(MUDRA,
Chögyam Trungpa,
Shambhala, Berkeley
and London,
1972.)

February 14

Of all the practices I know, the practice of *Tonglen,* Tibetan for "giving and receiving," is one of the most useful and powerful. When you feel yourself locked in upon yourself, Tonglen opens you to the truth of the suffering of others; when your heart is blocked, it destroys those forces that are obstructing it; and when you feel estranged from the person who is in pain before you, or bitter or despairing, it helps you to find within yourself and then to reveal the loving, expansive radiance of your own true nature. No other practice I know is as effective in destroying the self-grasping, self-cherishing, self-absorption of the ego, which is the root of all our suffering and all hard-heartedness.

Put very simply, the Tonglen practice of giving and receiving is to take on the suffering and pain of others and give to them your happiness, well-being, and peace of mind.

February 15

I know very well from my own experience how hard it is to imagine taking on the sufferings of others, and especially those of sick and dying people, without first building in yourself a strength and confidence of compassion. It is this strength and this confidence that will give your practice the power to transmute the suffering of others.

This is why I always recommend that you begin the Tonglen practice for others by first practicing it on yourself. Before you can send out love and compassion to others, you must uncover, deepen, create, and strengthen them in yourself, and heal yourself of any reticence or distress or anger or fear that might create an obstacle to practicing Tonglen wholeheartedly.

February 16

To integrate meditation in action is the whole ground and point and purpose of meditation. The violence and stress and the challenges and distractions of this modern life make this integration urgently necessary.

How do we achieve this integration, this permeation of everyday life with the calm humor and spacious detachment of meditation? There is no substitute for regular practice, for only through real practice will we begin to taste unbrokenly the calm of our nature of mind and so be able to sustain the experience of it in our everyday lives.

If you really wish to achieve this, what you need to do is practice not just as occasional medicine or therapy but as if it were your daily sustenance or food.

February 17

As we follow the teachings and as we practice, we will inevitably discover certain truths about ourselves that stand out prominently: There are places where we always get stuck; there are habitual patterns and strategies that are the legacy of negative karma, which we continuously repeat and reinforce; there are particular ways of seeing things—those tired old explanations of ourselves and the world around us—that are quite mistaken yet which we hold on to as authentic, and so distort our whole view of reality.

When we persevere on the spiritual path, and examine ourselves honestly, it begins to dawn on us more and more that our perceptions are nothing more than a web of illusions. Simply to acknowledge our confusion, even though we cannot accept it completely, can bring some light of understanding and spark off in us a new process, a process of healing.

February 18

We all have the karma to take one spiritual path or another, and I would encourage you, from the bottom of my heart, to follow with complete sincerity the path that inspires you most.

If you go on searching all the time, the searching itself becomes an obession and takes you over. You become a spiritual tourist, bustling about and never getting anywhere. As Patrul Rinpoche says: "You leave your elephant at home and look for its footprints in the forest." Following one teaching is not a way of confining you or jealously monopolizing you. It's a compassionate and practical way of keeping you centered and always on your path, despite all the obstacles that you, and the world, will inevitably present.

February 19

At the moment of death, there are two things that count: whatever we have done in our lives, and what state of mind we are in at that very moment. Even if we have accumulated a lot of negative karma, if we are able to make a real change of heart at the moment of death, it can decisively influence our future, and transform our karma, for the moment of death is an exceptionally powerful opportunity to purify karma.

A meditation technique used a great deal in Tibetan Buddhism is uniting the mind with the sound of a *mantra*. The definition of mantra is "that which protects the mind." That which protects the mind from negativity, or which protects you from your own mind, is mantra.

When you are nervous, disoriented, or emotionally fragile, inspired chanting or reciting of a mantra can change the state of your mind completely, by transforming its energy and atmosphere. How is this possible? Mantra is the essence of sound, the embodiment of the truth in the form of sound. Each syllable is impregnated with spiritual power, condenses a deep spiritual truth, and vibrates with the blessing of the speech of the buddhas. It is also said that the mind rides on the subtle energy of the breath, the prana, which moves through and purifies the subtle channels of the body. So when you chant a mantra, you are charging your breath and energy with the energy of the mantra, and so working directly on your mind and your subtle body.

February 21

The mantra I recommend to my students is:

OM AH HUM VAJRA GURU PADMA SIDDHI HUM

Tibetans say: "Om Ah Hung Benza Guru Péma Siddhi Hung," which is the mantra of Padmasambhava, the mantra of all the buddhas, masters, and realized beings, and is uniquely powerful for peace, for healing, for transformation, and for protection in this violent, chaotic age.

Recite the mantra quietly, with deep attention, and let your breath, the mantra, and your awareness slowly become one. Or chant it in an inspiring way, then rest in the profound silence that sometimes follows.

Why do we live in such terror of death? Perhaps the deepest reason why we are afraid of death is that we do not know who we are. We believe in a personal, unique, and separate identity; but if we dare to examine it, we find that this identity depends entirely on an endless collection of things to prop it up: our name, our "biography," our partners, family, home, job, friends, credit cards. . . . It is on their fragile and transient support that we rely for our security. So when they are all taken away, will we have any idea of who we really are?

We live under an assumed identity, in a neurotic fairy-tale world with no more reality than the Mock Turtle in *Alice in Wonderland.* Hypnotized by the thrill of building, we have raised the houses of our lives on sand.

This world can seem marvelously convincing until death collapses the illusion and evicts us from our hiding place. And what will happen to us then if we have no clue of any deeper reality?

February 23

Everything that we see around us is seen as it is because we have repeatedly solidified our experience of inner and outer reality in the same way, lifetime after lifetime, and this has led to the mistaken assumption that what we see is objectively real. In fact, as we go further along the spiritual path, we learn how to work directly with our fixed perceptions. All our old concepts of the world or of matter or of even ourselves are purified and dissolved, and an entirely new, what you could call "heavenly" field of vision and perception opens up. As William Blake said:

> *If the doors of perception were cleansed*
> *Everything would appear . . . as it is, infinite.*

February 24

Just as Buddha said that of all the buddhas who attained enlightenment, not one accomplished it without relying on the master, he also said: "It is only through devotion, and devotion alone, that you will realize the absolute truth."

So then, it is essential to know what real devotion is. It is not mindless adoration; it is not abdication of your responsibility to yourself, nor indiscriminately following of another's personality or whim. Real devotion is an unbroken receptivity to the truth. Real devotion is rooted in an awed and reverent gratitude, but one that is lucid, grounded, and intelligent.

February 25

As a Buddhist, I view death as a normal process, a reality that I accept will occur as long as I remain in this earthly existence. Knowing that I cannot escape it, I see no point in worrying about it. I tend to think of death as being like changing your clothes when they are old and worn out, rather than as some final end. Yet death is unpredictable: We do not know when or how it will take place. So it is only sensible to take certain precautions before it actually happens.

THE DALAI LAMA

February 26

In the Dzogchen teachings it is said that *your View and your posture* should be like a mountain.

Your View is the summation of your whole understanding and insight into the nature of mind, which you bring to your meditation. So your View translates into and inspires your posture, expressing the core of your being in the way you sit.

Sit, then, as if you were a mountain, with all its unshakable, steadfast majesty. A mountain is completely relaxed and at ease with itself, however strong the winds that batter it, however thick the dark clouds that swirl around its peak.

Sitting like a mountain, let your mind rise and fly and soar.

February 27

Ask yourself these two questions: Do I remember at every moment that I am dying, and that everyone and everything else is, and so treat all beings at all times with compassion? Has my understanding of death and impermanence become so keen and so urgent that I am devoting every second to the pursuit of enlightenment? If you can answer "yes" to both of these, *then* you *really* understand impermanence.

The whole point of Dzogchen meditation practice is to strengthen and stabilize Rigpa and allow it to grow to full maturity. The ordinary, habitual mind with its projections is extremely powerful. It keeps returning, and takes hold of us easily when we are inattentive or distracted.

As Dudjom Rinpoche used to say: "At present our Rigpa is like a little baby, stranded on the battlefield of strong arising thoughts." I like to say that we have to begin by babysitting our Rigpa, in the secure environment of meditation.

RIGPA

*The primordial, pure, pristine awareness which is
the innermost, essential nature of mind*

March 1

The practice of mindfulness unveils and reveals your essential Good Heart, because it dissolves and removes the unkindness or the harm in you. Only when you have removed the harm in yourself do you become truly useful to others. Through the practice, by slowly removing the unkindness and harm from yourself, you allow your true Good Heart, the fundamental goodness and kindness that are your real nature, to shine out and become the warm climate in which your true being flowers.

This is why I call meditation the true practice of peace, the true practice of nonaggression and nonviolence, and the real and greatest disarmament.

March 2

Whatever thoughts and emotions arise in meditation, allow them to rise and settle, like the waves in the ocean. Whatever you find yourself thinking, let that thought rise and settle, without any constraint. Don't grasp at it, feed it, or indulge it, don't cling to it, and don't try to solidify it. Neither follow thoughts nor invite them; be like the ocean looking at its own waves, or the sky gazing down on the clouds that pass across it.

You will soon find that thoughts are like the wind; they come and go. The secret is not to "think" about the thoughts but to allow them to flow through your mind, while keeping your mind free of afterthoughts.

March 3

I am now seventy-eight years old, and have seen so many, many things during my lifetime.

So many young people have died, so many people of my own age have died, so many old people have died. So many people that were high up have become low. So many people that were low have risen to be high up. So many countries have changed. There has been so much turmoil and tragedy, so many wars, and plagues, so much terrible destruction all over the world.

And yet all these changes are no more real than a dream. When you look deeply, you realize there is nothing that is permanent and constant, nothing, not even the tiniest hair on your body. And this is not a theory, but something you can actually come to know and realize and see, even, with your very own eyes.

DILGO KHYENTSE RINPOCHE

March 4

―――――――――

Buddha sat in serene and humble dignity on the ground, with the sky above him and around him, as if to show us that in meditation you sit with open, sky-like attitude of mind, yet remain present, earthed, and grounded. The sky is our absolute nature, which has no barriers and is boundless, and the ground is our reality, our relative, ordinary condition.

The posture we take when we meditate signifies that we are linking absolute and relative, sky and ground, heaven and earth, like two wings of a bird, integrating the skylike deathless nature of mind and the ground of our transient, mortal nature.

March 5

Anyone looking honestly at life will see that we live in a constant state of suspense and ambiguity. Our minds are perpetually shifting in and out of confusion and clarity. If we could be confused all the time, that would at least make for some kind of clarity. What is really baffling about life is that sometimes, despite all our confusion, we can also be really wise!

This constant uncertainty may make everything seem bleak and almost hopeless; but if you look more deeply at it, you will see that its very nature creates "gaps," spaces in which profound chances and opportunities for transformation are continuously flowering—if, that is, they can be seen and seized.

March 6

The nature of mind is the background to the whole of life and death, like the sky, which enfolds the whole universe in its embrace.

March 7

When we die we leave everything behind, especially this body we have cherished so much and relied upon so blindly and tried so hard to keep alive. But our minds are no more dependable than our bodies. Just look at your mind for a few minutes.

You will see that it is like a flea, constantly hopping to and fro. You will see that thoughts arise without any reason, without any connection. Swept along by the chaos of every moment, we are the victims of the fickleness of our minds. If this is the only state of consciousness we are familiar with, then to rely on our minds at the moment of death is an absurd gamble.

March 8

In his very first teaching, Buddha explained that the root cause of suffering is ignorance. But where exactly is this ignorance? And how does it display itself? Let's take an everyday example. Think about those people—we all know some—who are gifted with a remarkably powerful and sophisticated intelligence. Isn't it puzzling how, instead of helping them, as you might expect, it seems only to make them suffer more? It is almost as if their brilliance is directly responsible for their pain.

What is happening is quite clear: This intelligence of ours is captured and held hostage by ignorance, which then makes use of it freely for its own ends. This is how we can be extraordinarily intelligent and yet absolutely wrong, at one and the same time.

March 9

Sometimes we have fleeting glimpses of the nature of mind. These can be inspired by an exalting piece of music, by the serene happiness we sometimes feel in nature, or by the most ordinary everyday situation. They can arise simply while watching snow slowly drifting down, or seeing the sun rising behind a mountain, or watching a shaft of light falling into a room in a mysteriously moving way. Such moments of illumination, peace, and bliss happen to us all and stay strangely with us.

I think we do, sometimes, half understand these glimpses. But then, modern culture gives us no context or framework in which to comprehend them. Worse still, rather than encouraging us to explore them more deeply and discover where they spring from, we are told in both obvious and subtle ways to shut them out. We know that no one will take us seriously if we try to share them. So we ignore what could be really the most revealing experiences of our lives, if only we understood them. This is perhaps the darkest and most disturbing aspect of modern civilization—its ignorance and repression of *who we really are.*

Know all things to be like this:
A mirage, a cloud castle,
A dream, an apparition,
Without essence, but with qualities that can be seen.

Know all things to be like this:
As the moon in a bright sky
In some clear lake reflected,
Though to that lake the moon has never moved.

Know all things to be like this:
As an echo that derives
From music, sounds, and weeping,
Yet in that echo is no melody.

Know all things to be like this:
As a magician makes illusions
Of horses, oxen, carts and other things,
Nothing is as it appears.

BUDDHA

March 11

Compassion is the best protection; it is also, as the great masters of the past have always known, the source of all healing. Suppose you have a disease such as cancer or AIDS. By taking on the sickness of those suffering like you, in addition to your own pain, with a mind full of compassion, you will—beyond any doubt—purify the past negative karma that is the cause, now and in the future, of the continuation of your suffering.

In Tibet there have been many extraordinary cases of people who, when they heard they were dying of a terminal illness, gave away everything they had and went to the cemetery to die. There they practiced taking on the suffering of others; and what is amazing is that instead of dying, they returned home, fully healed.

March 12

Although the results of our actions may not have matured yet, they will inevitably ripen, given the right conditions. Usually we forget what we do, and it is only long afterward that the results catch up with us. By then we are unable to connect them with their causes. "Imagine an eagle," says Jikmé Lingpa. "It is flying, high in the sky. It casts no shadow. Nothing shows that it is there. Then suddenly it spies its prey, dives, and swoops to the ground. And as it drops, its menacing shadow appears."

March 13

The preliminary training of meditation practice and purification ripens and opens the student's heart and mind to the direct understanding of the truth.

Then, in the powerful moment of introduction, the master can direct his realization of the nature of mind— what we call the master's "wisdom mind"—into the mind of the now authentically receptive student.

The master is doing nothing less than introducing the student to what the Buddha actually *is,* awakening the student to the living presence of enlightenment within. In that experience, the Buddha, the nature of mind, and the master's wisdom mind are all fused into, and revealed as, one. The student then recognizes, in a blaze of gratitude, beyond any shadow of doubt, that there is not, has never been, and could not ever be any separation: between student and master, between the master's wisdom mind and the nature of the student's mind.

March 14

The nature of everything is illusory and ephemeral,
Those with dualistic perception regard suffering as
    happiness,
Like they who lick the honey from a razor's edge.
How pitiful they who cling strongly to concrete reality:
Turn your attention within, my heart friends.

NYOSHUH KHEN RINPOCHE

March 15

On that momentous night when Buddha attained enlightenment, it is said that he went through several different stages of awakening. In the first, with his mind "collected and purified, without blemish, free of defilements, grown soft, workable, fixed and immovable," he turned his attention to the recollection of his previous lives. This is what he tells us of that experience:

I remembered many, many former existences I had passed through: one, two births, three, four, five . . . fifty, one hundred . . . a hundred thousand, in various world-periods. I knew everything about these various births: where they had taken place, what my name had been, which family I had been born into, and what I had done. I lived through again the good and bad fortune of each life and my death in each life, and came to life again and again. In this way I recalled innumerable previous existences with their exact characteristic features and circumstances. This knowledge I gained in the first watch of the night.

March 16

Lifetimes of ignorance have brought us to identify the whole of our being with ego. Its greatest triumph is to inveigle us into believing its best interests are our best interests, and even into identifying our very survival with its own. This is a savage irony, considering that ego and its grasping are at the root of all our suffering.

Yet, ego is so terribly convincing, and we have been its dupe for so long, that the thought that we might ever become egoless terrifies us. To be egoless, ego whispers to us, is to lose all the rich romance of being human, to be reduced to a colorless robot or a brain-dead vegetable.

March 17

The extraordinary qualities of great beings who hide their nature escapes ordinary people like us, despite our best efforts in examining them. On the other hand, even ordinary charlatans are expert at deceiving others by behaving like saints.

PATRUL RINPOCHE

March 18

As you continue to meditate on compassion, when you see someone suffer, your first response becomes not mere pity but deep compassion. You feel for that person respect and even gratitude, because you now know that whoever prompts you to develop compassion by his or her suffering is in fact giving you one of the greatest gifts of all, as you are being helped to develop that very quality you need most in your progress toward enlightenment.

That is why we say in Tibet that the beggar who is asking you for money, or the sick, old woman wringing your heart, may be the buddhas in disguise, manifesting on your path to help you grow in compassion and so move toward buddhahood.

March 19

I always tell my students not to come out of meditation too quickly. Allow a period of some minutes for
the peace of the practice of meditation to infiltrate your
life. As my master, Dudjom Rinpoche, said: "Don't
jump up and rush off, but mingle your mindfulness
with everyday life. Be like a man who's fractured his
skull, always careful in case someone will touch him."

March 20

At the moment of death, our state of mind is all-important. If we die in a positive frame of mind, we can improve our next birth, despite our negative karma. And if we are upset and distressed, it may have a detrimental effect, even though we may have used our lives well. This means that *the last thought and emotion that we have before we die has an extremely powerful determining effect on our immediate future.*

This is why the masters stress that the quality of the atmosphere around us when we die is crucial. With our friends and relatives, we should do all we can to inspire positive emotions and sacred feelings, like love, compassion, and devotion, and all we can to help them to "let go of grasping, yearning, and attachment."

The most important thing is not to get trapped in what I see everywhere in the West, a "shopping mentality": shopping around from master to master, teaching to teaching, without any continuity or real, sustained dedication to any one discipline. Nearly all the great spiritual masters of all traditions agree that the essential thing is to master one way, one path to the truth, by following one tradition with all your heart and mind to the end of the spiritual journey, while, of course, remaining open and respectful toward the insights of all others. In Tibet we used to say: "knowing one, you accomplish all." The modern faddish idea that we can always keep all our options open and so never need commit ourselves to anything is one of the greatest and most dangerous delusions of our culture, and one of ego's most effective ways of sabotaging our spiritual search.

March 22

The practice of mindfulness defuses our negativity, aggression, and turbulent emotions, which may have been gathering power over many lifetimes. Rather than suppressing emotions or indulging in them, here it is important to view them—your thoughts and whatever arises—with an acceptance and generosity that are as open and spacious as possible. Tibetan masters say that this wise generosity has the flavor of boundless space, so warm and cozy that you feel enveloped and protected by it, as if by a blanket of sunlight.

March 23

The master is like a great ship for beings to cross the perilous ocean of existence, an unerring captain who guides them to the dry land of liberation, a rain that extinguishes the fire of the passions, a bright sun and moon that dispel the darkness of ignorance, a firm ground that can bear the weight of both good and bad, a wish-fulfilling tree that bestows temporal happiness and ultimate bliss, a treasury of vast and deep instructions, a wish-fulfilling jewel granting all the qualities of realization, a father and a mother giving their love equally to all sentient beings, a great river of compassion, a mountain rising above worldly concerns unshaken by the winds of emotions, and a great cloud filled with rain to soothe the torments of the passions.

"In brief, he is the equal of all the buddhas. To make any connection with him, whether through seeing him, hearing his voice, remembering him, or being touched by his hand, will lead us toward liberation. To have full confidence in him is the sure way to progress toward enlightenment. The warmth of his wisdom and compassion will melt the ore of our being and release the gold of the buddha-nature within.

DILGO KHYENTSE RINPOCHE

March 24

For most of us, karma and negative emotions obscure the ability to see our own intrinsic nature, and the nature of reality. As a result we clutch on to happiness and suffering as real, and in our unskillful and ignorant actions go on sowing the seeds of our next birth. Our actions keep us bound to the continuous cycle of worldly existence, to the endless round of birth and death. So *everything is at risk in how we live now at this very moment: How we live now can cost us our entire future.*

This is the real and urgent reason why we must prepare now to meet death wisely, to transform our karmic future, and to avoid the tragedy of falling into delusion again and again and repeating the painful round of birth and death. This life is the only time and place we can prepare in, and we can only truly prepare through spiritual practice: This is the inescapable message of the natural bardo of this life.

March 25

Enlightenment for Gautama [the Buddha] felt as though a prison which had confined him for thousands of lifetimes had broken open. Ignorance had been the jailkeeper. Because of ignorance, his mind had been obscured, just like the moon and stars hidden by the storm clouds. Clouded by endless waves of deluded thoughts, the mind had falsely divided reality into subject and object, self and others, existence and non-existence, birth and death, and from these discriminations arose wrong views—the prisons of feelings, craving, grasping, and becoming. The suffering of birth, old age, sickness, and death only made the prison walls thicker. The only thing to do was to seize the jailkeeper and see his true face. The jailkeeper was ignorance. . . . Once the jailkeeper was gone, the jail would disappear and never be rebuilt again.

THICH NHAT HANH
THE BUDDHA'S ENLIGHTENMENT

March 26

It is extremely hard to rest undistracted in the nature of mind, even for a moment, let alone to self-liberate a single thought or emotion as it rises. We often assume that simply because we understand something intellectually, or think we do, we have actually realized it. This is a great delusion. It requires the maturity that only years of listening, contemplation, reflection, meditation, and sustained practice can ripen.

March 27

There is no swifter, more moving, or more powerful practice for invoking the help of the enlightened beings, for arousing devotion and realizing the nature of mind, than the practice of Guru Yoga. Dilgo Khyentse Rinpoche wrote: "The words Guru Yoga mean 'union with the nature of the guru,'" and in this practice we are given methods by which we can blend our own minds with the enlightened mind of the master.

The master—the guru—embodies the crystallization of the blessings of all buddhas, masters, and enlightened beings. So to invoke him or her is to invoke them all; and to merge your mind and heart with your master's wisdom mind is to merge your mind with the truth and very embodiment of enlightenment.

March 28

As Buddha himself was passing away, he prophesied that Padmasambhava would be born not long after his death in order to spread the teaching of the Tantras. It was Padmasambhava who established Buddhism in Tibet in the eighth century. For us Tibetans, Padmasambhava, Guru Rinpoche, embodies a cosmic, timeless principle; he is the universal master.

I have always turned to Padmasambhava in times of difficulty and crisis, and his blessing and power have never failed me. When I think of him, all my masters are embodied in him. To me he is completely alive at all moments, and the whole universe, at each moment, shines with his beauty, strength, and presence.

March 29

Taking impermanence truly to heart is to be slowly freed from the idea of grasping, from our flawed and destructive view of permanence, from the false passion for security on which we have built everything. Slowly it dawns on us that all the heartache we have been through from grasping at the ungraspable was, in the deepest sense, unnecessary.

At the beginning this too may be painful to accept, because it seems so unfamiliar. But as we reflect, slowly our hearts and minds go through a gradual transformation. Letting go begins to feel more natural, and becomes easier and easier.

It may take a long time for the extent of our foolishness to sink in, but the more we reflect, the more we develop the view of letting go. It is then that a complete shift takes place in our way of looking at everything.

March 30

We cannot hope to die peacefully if our lives have been full of violence, or if our minds have mostly been agitated by emotions like anger, attachment, or fear. So if we wish to die well, we must learn how to live well: Hoping for a peaceful death, we must cultivate peace in our mind, and in our way of life.

THE DALAI LAMA

March 31

The most essential point of the meditation posture is to keep the back straight, like "an arrow" or "a pile of golden coins." The "inner energy," or *prana,* will then flow easily through the subtle channels of the body, and your mind will find its true state of rest. Don't force anything. The lower part of the spine has a natural curve; it should be relaxed but upright. Your head should be balanced comfortably on your neck. It is your shoulders and the upper part of your torso that carry the strength and grace of the posture, and they should be held in strong poise, but without any tension.

Sit with your legs crossed. You do not have to sit in the "full-lotus" posture, which is emphasized more in advanced yoga practice. The crossed legs express the unity of life and death, good and bad, skillful means and wisdom, masculine and feminine principles, samsara and nirvana, and the humor of nonduality. Rest your hands comfortably covering your knees. This is called the "mind in comfort and ease" posture. If you prefer to sit on a chair, keep your legs relaxed, and be sure always to keep your back straight.

GOM
Meditation

April 1

Since everything is but an apparition,
Perfect in being what it is,
Having nothing to do with good or bad,
Acceptance or rejection
You might as well burst out laughing!

LONGCHENPA

April 2

Just as a writer learns the spontaneous freedom of expression only after years of often grueling study, and just as the simple grace of a dancer is achieved only with enormous, patient effort, so when you begin to understand where meditation will lead you, you will approach it as the greatest endeavor of your life, one that demands of you the deepest perseverance, enthusiasm, intelligence, and discipline.

At the time of Buddha, there lived an old beggar woman called Relying on Joy. She used to watch the kings, princes, and people making offerings to Buddha and his disciples, and there was nothing she would have liked more than to be able to do the same. But she could only beg enough oil to fill a single lamp. However, as she placed it before Buddha she made this wish: "I have nothing to offer but this tiny lamp. But through this offering, in the future may I be blessed with the lamp of wisdom. May I free all beings from their darkness. May I purify all their obscurations, and lead them to enlightenment."

That night, the oil in all the other lamps went out. But the beggar woman's lamp was still burning at dawn, when Buddha's great disciple Maudgalyayana came to collect the lamps. He saw no reason why one lamp was still alight and tried to snuff it out. But whatever he did, the lamp kept burning.

Buddha had been watching all along, and said: "Maudgalyayana, do you want to put out that lamp? You cannot. You could not even move it, let alone put it out. If you were to pour the water from all the oceans over this lamp, it still wouldn't go out. The water in all the rivers and lakes of the world could not extinguish it. Why not? Because this lamp was offered with devotion, and with purity of heart and mind. And that motivation has made it of tremendous benefit."

April 4

Sometime, somewhere you need to take something to be the truth. But if you cling to it too strongly, then even when the truth comes in person and knocks on your door, you will not open it.

BUDDHA

Visualize someone to whom you feel very close, particularly someone who is suffering and in pain. As you breathe in, imagine you take in all their suffering and pain with compassion, and as you breathe out, send your warmth, healing, love, joy, and happiness streaming out to them.

Now, gradually widen the circle of your compassion to embrace first other people to whom you also feel very close, then to those about whom you feel indifferent, then to those whom you dislike or have difficulty with, then even to those whom you feel are actively monstrous and cruel. Allow your compassion to become universal, and to enfold in its embrace all sentient beings, and all beings, in fact, without any exception.

April 6

In the ordinary mind, we perceive the stream of thoughts as continuous, but in reality this is not the case. You will discover for yourself that there is a gap between each thought. When the past thought is past, and the future thought has not yet arisen, you will always find a gap in which the Rigpa, the nature of mind, is revealed. So the work of meditation is to allow thoughts to slow down, to make that gap become more and more apparent.

April 7

Even Buddha died. His death was a teaching, to shock the naive, the indolent, and the complacent, to wake us up to the truth that everything is impermanent and death an inescapable fact of life. As he was approaching death, Buddha said:

> *Of all footprints*
> *That of the elephant is supreme.*
> *Of all mindfulness meditations*
> *That on death is supreme.*

Because life is nothing but a perpetual fluctuation of birth, death, and transition, so bardo experiences are happening to us all the time, and are a basic part of our psychological makeup. Normally, however, we are oblivious to the bardos and their gaps, as our mind passes from one so-called solid situation to the next, habitually ignoring the transitions that are always occurring.

In fact, as the teachings can help us to understand, every moment of our experience is a bardo, as each thought and each emotion arises out of, and dies back into, the essence of mind. It is in moments of strong change and transition especially, the teachings make us aware, that the true skylike, primordial nature of mind will have a chance to manifest.

April 9

We have been taught to spend our lives chasing our thoughts and projections. Even when "mind" is talked about, it is only thoughts and emotions that are referred to; and when our researchers study what they imagine to be the mind, they look only at its projections. No one ever really looks into the mind itself, the ground from which all these expressions arise; and this has tragic consequences.

April 10

There are rough as well as gentle waves in the ocean; strong emotions come, like anger, desire, jealousy. The real practitioner recognizes them not as a disturbance or an obstacle but as a great opportunity. The fact that you react to arisings such as these with habitual tendencies of attachment and aversion is a sign not only that you are distracted but that you do not have the recognition and have lost the ground of Rigpa. To react to emotions in this way empowers them and binds you even tighter in the chains of delusion.

The great secret of Dzogchen is to see right through them, as soon as they arise, to what they really are: the vivid and electric manifestation of the energy of Rigpa itself. As you gradually learn to do this, even the most turbulent emotions fail to seize hold of you and instead dissolve, as wild waves rise and rear and sink back into the calm of the ocean.

April 11

Wrong views and wrong convictions can be the most devastating of all our delusions. Surely Adolf Hitler and Pol Pot must have been convinced that they were right too? And yet each and every one of us has that same dangerous tendency as they had: to form convictions, believe them without question, and act on them, so bringing down suffering not only on ourselves but on all those around us.

On the other hand, the heart of Buddha's teaching is to see *"the actual state of things, as they are,"* and this is called *the true View*. It is a view that is all-embracing, as the role of spiritual teachings is precisely to give us a *complete* perspective on the nature of mind and reality.

April 12

What should we "do" with the mind in meditation? Nothing at all.

Just leave it, simply, as it is.

One master described meditation as "mind, suspended in space, nowhere."

April 13

There are those who look on death with a naive, thoughtless cheerfulness, thinking that for some unknown reason death will work out all right for them, and that it is nothing to worry about. When I think of them, I am reminded of what one Tibetan master says: "People often make the mistake of being frivolous about death and think, 'Oh well, death happens to everybody. It's not a big deal, it's natural. I'll be fine.'" That's a nice theory until one is dying.

April 14

Every subatomic interaction consists of the annihilation of the original particles and the creation of new subatomic particles. The subatomic world is a continual dance of creation and annihilation, of mass changing into energy and energy changing to mass. Transient forms sparkle in and out of existence, creating a never-ending, forever newly created reality.

GARY ZUKAV

April 15

From a Buddhist point of view, the actual experience of death is very important. Although how or where we will be reborn is generally dependent on karmic forces, our state of mind at the time of death can influence the quality of our next rebirth. So at the moment of death, in spite of the great variety of karmas we have accumulated, if we make a special effort to generate a virtuous state of mind, we may strengthen and activate a virtuous karma, and so bring about a happy rebirth.

THE DALAI LAMA

April 16

Even within the human realm, all of us have our own individual karma. Human beings look much the same, but we perceive things utterly differently, and we each live in our own unique, separate, individual world. As Kalu Rinpoche says:

"If a hundred people sleep and dream, each of them will experience a different world in his dream. Everyone's dream might be said to be true, but it would be meaningless to ascertain that only one person's dream was the true world and all others were fallacies. There is truth for each perceiver according to the karmic patterns conditioning his perceptions."

April 17

Rest in natural great peace
This exhausted mind
Beaten helpless by karma and neurotic thought,
Like the relentless fury of the pounding waves
In the infinite ocean of samsara.

Rest in natural great peace.

NYOSHUH KHENPO RINPOCHE

April 18

To contemplate impermanence on its own is not enough: You have to work with it in your life. Let's try an experiment. Pick up a coin. Imagine that it represents the object at which you are grasping. Hold it tightly clutched in your fist and extend your arm, with the palm of your hand facing the ground. Now if you let go or relax your grip, you will lose what you are clinging on to. That's why you hold on.

But there's another possibility: You *can* let go and yet keep hold of it. With your arm still outstretched, turn your hand over so that it faces the sky. Release your hand and the coin still rests on your open palm. You let go. And the coin is still yours, even with all this space around it.

So there *is* a way in which we can accept impermanence and still relish life, at one and the same time, without grasping.

Above all else, we need to nourish our true self—
what we can call our buddha nature—for so often we
make the fatal mistake of identifying with our confusion, and then using it to judge and condemn ourselves,
which feeds the lack of self-love that so many of us
suffer from today.

How vital it is to refrain from the temptation to
judge ourselves or the teachings, and to be humorously
aware of our condition, and to realize that we are, at
the moment, as if many people all living in one person.

And how encouraging it can be to accept that from
one perspective we all have huge problems, which we
bring to the spiritual path and which indeed may have
led us to the teachings, and yet to know from another
point of view that ultimately our problems are not so
real or so solid, or so insurmountable as we have told
ourselves.

April 20

If all we know of mind is the aspect of mind that dissolves when we die, we will be left with no idea of what continues, no knowledge of the new dimension of the deeper reality of the nature of mind. So it is vital for us all to familiarize ourselves with the nature of mind while we are still alive. Only then will we be prepared for the time when it reveals itself spontaneously and powerfully at the moment of death; be able to recognize it "as naturally," the teachings say, "as a child running into its mother's lap"; and by remaining in that state, finally be liberated.

April 21

Ego plays brilliantly on our fundamental fear of losing control, and of the unknown. We might say to ourselves: "I should really let go of ego, I'm in such pain; but if I do, what's going to happen to me?"

Ego will chime in sweetly: "I know I'm sometimes a nuisance, and believe me, I quite understand if you want me to leave. But is that really what you want? Think: If I do go, what's going to happen to you? Who'll look after you? Who will protect and care for you like I've done all these years?"

Even if we see through the lies of the ego, we are just too scared to abandon it; for without any true knowledge of the nature of our mind, or true identity, we simply have no other alternative. Again and again we cave in to ego's demands with the same sad self-hatred as the alcoholic feels reaching for the drink that he knows is destroying him, or the drug addict feels groping for the drug that she knows after a brief high will only leave her flat and desperate.

April 22

Don't be in too much of a hurry to solve all your doubts and problems. As the masters say: "Make haste slowly." I always tell my students not to have unreasonable expectations, because it takes time for spiritual growth. It takes years to learn Japanese properly or to become a doctor. Can we really expect to have all the answers, let alone become enlightened, in a few weeks?

The spiritual journey is one of continuous learning and purification. When you know this, you become humble. There is a famous Tibetan saying: "Do not mistake understanding for realization, and do not mistake realization for liberation." And Milarepa said: "Do not entertain hopes for realization, but practice all your life."

April 23

ON BODHICITTA:
The Compassionate Heart of the Enlightened Mind

It is the supreme elixir
That overcomes the sovereignty of death.
It is the inexhaustible treasure
That eliminates poverty in the world.
It is the supreme medicine
That quells the world's disease.
It is the tree that shelters all beings
Wandering and tired on the path of conditioned
*   existence.*
It is the universal bridge
That leads to freedom from unhappy states of birth.
It is the dawning moon of the mind
That dispels the torment of disturbing conceptions.
It is the great sun that finally removes
The misty ignorance of the world.

SHANTIDEVA

After meditation, it's important not to give in to our tendency to solidify the way we perceive things.

When you do re-enter everyday life, let the wisdom, insight, compassion, humor, fluidity, spaciousness, and detachment that meditation brought you pervade your day-to-day experience. Meditation awakens in you the realization of how the nature of everything is illusory and dreamlike. Maintain that awareness even in the thick of samsara.

One great master has said: "After meditation practice, one should become a child of illusion."

At present, our body is undoubtedly the center of our whole universe. We associate it, without thinking, with our self and our ego, and this thoughtless and false association continually reinforces our illusion of their inseparable, concrete existence. Because our body seems so convincingly to exist, our "I" seems to exist, and "you" seem to exist, and the entire illusory, dualistic world we never stop projecting around us looks ultimately solid and real.

When we die, this whole compound construction falls dramatically to pieces.

April 26

Dudjom Rinpoche says of the moment when Rigpa is directly revealed: "That moment is like taking a hood off your head. What boundless spaciousness and relief! This is the supreme seeing: seeing what was not seen before." When you "see what was not seen before," everything opens, expands, and becomes crisp, clear, brimming with life vivid with wonder and freshness. It is as if the roof of your mind were flying off, or a flock of birds suddenly took off from a dark nest. All limitations dissolve and fall away, as if, the Tibetans say, a seal were broken open.

April 27

There is a danger, called in the tradition "losing the Action in the View." A teaching as high and powerful as Dzogchen entails an extreme risk. Deluding yourself that you are liberating your thoughts and emotions, when in fact you are nowhere near able to do so, and thinking that you are acting with the spontaneity of a true Dzogchen yogi, all you are doing is simply accumulating vast amounts of negative karma. As Padmasambhava says, and this is the attitude we all should have:

> Though my View is as spacious as the sky,
> My actions and respect for cause and effect are as fine
>   as grains of flour.

April 28

Dudjom Rinpoche used to say that a beginner should practice meditation in short sessions. Practice for four or five minutes, then take a short break of just one minute. During the break, let go of the method, but do not let go of your mindfulness altogether.

Sometimes when you have been struggling to practice, curiously, the very moment when you take a break from the method—if you are still mindful and present—is the moment when meditation actually happens. That is why the break is just as important a part of meditation as the sitting itself. Sometimes I tell my students who are having problems with their practice to practice during the break and take a break during their meditation!

April 29

Gampopa, Milarepa's greatest disciple, asked him at the moment of their parting: "When will be the time for me to start guiding students?" Milarepa replied: "When you are not like you are now, when your whole perception has been transformed, and you are able to see, really see, this old man before you as nothing less than the Buddha himself. When devotion has brought you to that moment of recognition, that moment will be the sign that the time for you to teach has come."

It is my devotion to my masters that gives me the strength to teach, and the openness and receptivity to learn, and go on learning. Dilgo Khyentse Rinpoche himself never stopped humbly receiving teachings from other masters, and often from those who were his own disciples. The devotion that gives the inspiration to teach, then, is also the devotion that gives the humility to go on learning.

April 30

Now when the bardo of this life is dawning upon me,
I will abandon laziness for which life has no time,
Enter, undistracted, the path of listening and hearing,
    reflection and contemplation, and meditation,
Making perceptions and mind the path, and realize the
    "three kayas": the enlightened mind;
Now that I have once attained a human body,
There is no time on the path for the mind to wander.

PADMASAMBHAVA

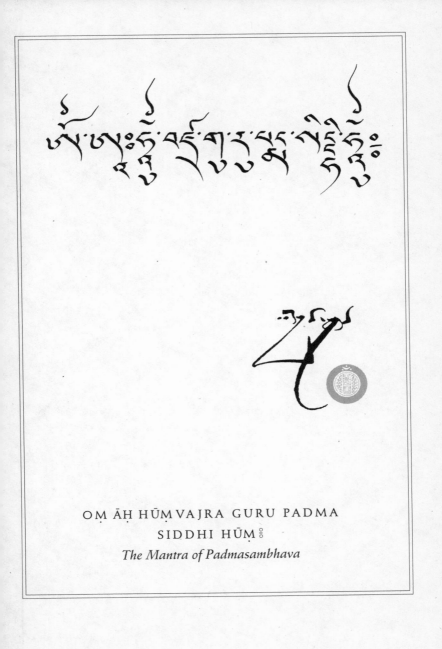

OM ĀḤ HŪṂ VAJRA GURU PADMA
SIDDHI HŪṂ ॐ
The Mantra of Padmasambhava

May 1

"If you spent one-tenth of the time you devoted to distractions like chasing women or making money to spiritual practice, you would be enlightened in a few years!"

RAMAKRISHNA

May 2

There is a famous saying: "If the mind is not contrived, it is spontaneously blissful, just as water, when not agitated, is by nature transparent and clear."

I often compare the mind in meditation to a jar of muddy water: The more we leave the water without interfering or stirring it, the more the particles of dirt will sink to the bottom, letting the natural clarity of the water shine through. The very nature of the mind is such that if you only leave it in its unaltered and natural state, it will find its true nature, which is bliss and clarity.

May 3

The gods are said to live lives of fabulous luxury, reveling in every conceivable pleasure, without a thought for the spiritual dimension of life. All seems to go well until death draws near, and unexpected signs of decay appear. Then the gods' wives and lovers no longer dare approach them, but throw flowers to them from a distance, with casual prayers that they be reborn again as gods. None of their memories of happiness or comfort can shelter them now from the suffering they face; they only make it more savage. So the dying gods are left to die alone in misery.

The fate of the gods reminds me of the way the elderly, the sick, and the dying are treated today. Our society is obsessed with youth, sex, and power, and we shun old age and decay. Isn't it terrifying that we discard old people when their working life is finished and they are no longer useful? Isn't it disturbing that we cast them into old people's homes, where they die lonely and abandoned?

Listening is a far more difficult process than most people imagine. Really to listen in the way that is meant by the masters is to let go utterly of ourselves, to let go of all the information, all the concepts, all the ideas, and all the prejudices that our heads are stuffed with. If you really listen to the teachings, those concepts, which are our real hindrance—the one thing that stands between us and our true nature—can slowly and steadily be washed away.

May 5

If you were to draw one essential message from the fact of reincarnation, it would be: Develop a good heart that longs for other beings to find lasting happiness, and acts to secure that happiness. Nourish and practice kindness.

The Dalai Lama has said: "There is no need for temples; no need for complicated philosophy. Our own brain, our own heart is our temple; my philosophy is kindness."

May 6

I adopted the theory of reincarnation when I was twenty-six. Religion offered nothing to the point. Even work could not give me complete satisfaction. Work is futile if we cannot utilize the experience we collect in one life in the next. When I discovered reincarnation . . . time was no longer limited. I was no longer a slave to the hands of the clock. . . . I would like to communicate to others the calmness that the long view of life gives to us.

HENRY FORD

May 7

Imagine you are sitting in front of a glass door that leads out into your garden, looking through it, gazing out into space. It seems as though there is nothing between you and the sky, because you cannot see the surface of the glass. You would bang your nose if you got up and tried to walk through, thinking it wasn't there. But if you touch it you will see at once that there is something there that holds your fingerprints, something that comes between you and the space outside.

In the same manner, the ground of the ordinary mind prevents us from breaking through to the skylike nature of our mind, even if we can still have glimpses of it. We have to break out of the ground of the ordinary mind altogether, to discover and let in the fresh air of Rigpa.

Even though that which is usually called "mind" is widely esteemed and much discussed,

Still it is not understood or it is wrongly understood or it is understood in a one-sided manner only.

Since it is not understood correctly, *just as it is in itself,*

There comes into existence inconceivable numbers of philosophical ideas and assertions.

Furthermore, since ordinary individuals do not understand it,

They do not recognize their own nature,

And so they continue to wander among the six destinies of rebirth within the three worlds, and thus experience suffering.

Therefore, not understanding your own mind is a very grievous fault.

PADMASAMBHAVA

May 9

When you practice, say you find yourself in a deep state of stillness; often it does not last very long as a thought or a movement always arises, like a wave in the ocean. Don't reject the movement or particularly embrace the stillness, but continue the flow of your pure presence. The pervasive, peaceful state of your meditation is the Rigpa itself, and all risings are none other than this Rigpa's self-radiance. This is the heart and the basis of Dzogchen practice.

One way to imagine this is as if you were riding on the sun's rays back to the sun: You trace the risings back, at once, to their very root, the ground of Rigpa. As you embody the steadfast stability of the View, you are no longer deceived and distracted by whatever rises, and so cannot fall prey to delusion.

May 10

The absolute truth cannot be realized within the domain of the ordinary mind. And the path beyond the ordinary mind, all the great wisdom traditions have told us, is through the heart. This path of the heart is devotion.

May 11

To meditate is to make a complete break with how we "normally" operate, for it is a state free of all cares and concerns, in which there is no competition, no desire to possess or grasp at anything, no intense and anxious struggle, and no hunger to achieve: an ambitionless state where there is neither acceptance nor rejection, neither hope nor fear, a state in which we slowly begin to release all those emotions and concepts that have imprisoned us into the space of natural simplicity.

May 12

Always recognize the dreamlike qualities of life and reduce attachment and aversion. Practice good-heartedness toward all beings. Be loving and compassionate, no matter what others do to you. What they will do will not matter so much when you see it as a dream. The trick is to have positive intention during the dream. This is the essential point. This is true spirituality.

CHAKDUD TULKU RINPOCHE

May 13

Death is a vast mystery, but there are two things we can say about it: *It is absolutely certain that we will die,* and *it is uncertain when or how we will die.* The only surety we have, then, is this uncertainty about the hour of our death, which we seize on as the excuse to postpone facing death directly. We are like children who cover their eyes in a game of hide and seek and think that no one can see them.

May 14

If meditation in Dzogchen is simply to continue the flow of Rigpa after the introduction by the master, how do we know when it is Rigpa and when it is not? I asked Dilgo Khyentse Rinpoche this question, and he replied with his characteristic simplicity: "If you are in an unaltered state, it is Rigpa."

If we are not contriving or manipulating the mind in any way, but simply resting in an unaltered state of pure and pristine awareness, that *is* Rigpa. If there is any contriving on our part or any kind of manipulating or grasping, it is not. Rigpa is a state in which there is no longer any doubt; there is not really a mind to doubt: you see directly. If you are in this state, a complete, natural certainty and confidence surge up with the Rigpa itself, and that is how you know.

May 15

Renunciation has both sadness and joy in it: sadness because you realize the futility of your old ways, and joy because of the greater vision that begins to unfold when you are able to let go of them. This is no ordinary joy. It is a joy that gives birth to a new and profound strength, a confidence, an abiding inspiration that comes from the realization that you are not condemned to your habits, that you *can* indeed emerge from them, that you *can* change, and grow more and more free.

May 16

Whatever joy there is in this world
All comes from desiring others to be happy,
And whatever suffering there is in this world
All comes from desiring myself to be happy.

SHANTIDEVA

May 17

In the Dzogchen teachings it is said that your meditation and your gaze should be like the vast expanse of a great ocean: all-pervading, open, and limitless. Just as your View and posture are inseparable, so your meditation inspires your gaze, and they now merge as one.

Do not focus on anything in particular; instead, turn back into yourself slightly, and let your gaze expand and become more and more spacious and pervasive. You will discover now that your vision itself becomes more expansive, and that there is more peace, more compassion in your gaze, more equanimity, and more poise.

May 18

========================

*After all, it is no more surprising to be born twice than it
is to be born once.*

VOLTAIRE

"If we have lived before," I'm often asked, "why
don't we remember it?" But why should the fact that
we cannot remember our past lives mean that we have
never lived before? After all, experiences—of our childhood, or of yesterday, or even of what we were thinking an hour ago—were vivid as they occurred, but the
memory of them has almost totally eroded, as though
they had never taken place. If we cannot remember
what we were doing or thinking last Monday, how on
earth do we imagine it would be easy, or normal, to remember what we were doing in a previous lifetime?

To end the bizarre tyranny of ego is why we take the spiritual path, but the resourcefulness of ego is almost infinite, and it can at every stage sabotage and pervert our desire to be free of it. The truth is simple, and the teachings are extremely clear; but I have seen again and again, with great sadness, that as soon as they begin to touch and move us, ego tries to complicate them, because it knows it is fundamentally threatened.

However hard ego may try to sabotage the spiritual path, if you really continue on it, and work deeply with the practice of meditation, you will begin slowly to realize just how gulled you have been by ego's promises: false hopes and false fears. Slowly you begin to understand that both hope and fear are enemies of your peace of mind; hopes deceive you, and leave you empty and disappointed, and fears paralyze you in the narrow cell of your false identity. You begin to see also just how all-encompassing the sway of ego has been over your mind, and in the space of freedom opened up by meditation, when you are momentarily released from grasping, you glimpse the exhilarating spaciousness of your true nature.

May 20

The times when you are suffering can be those when you are open, and where you are extremely vulnerable can be where your greatest strength really lies.

Say to yourself: "I am not going to run away from this suffering. I want to use it in the best and richest way I can, so that I can become more compassionate and more helpful to others." Suffering, after all, can teach us about compassion. If you suffer, you will know how it is when others suffer. And if you are in a position to help others, it is through your suffering that you will find the understanding and compassion to do so.

Sometimes when we see too much truth about ourselves suddenly mirrored in front of us by the teacher or the teachings, it is simply too difficult to face, too terrifying to recognize, too painful to accept as the reality about ourselves. We deny and reject it, in an absurd and desperate attempt to defend ourselves from *ourselves*, from the truth of who we really are. And when there are things too powerful or too difficult to accept about ourselves, we project them onto the world around us, usually onto those who help us and love us the most—our teacher, the teachings, our parent, or our closest friend.

How can we possibly penetrate the tough shield of this defensive system? The very best solution is when we can recognize ourselves that we are living duped by our own delusions. I have seen how for many people a glimpse of the truth, the true View, can bring the whole fantastic construction of wrong views, fabricated by ignorance, tumbling instantly to the ground.

May 22

In a sense everything is dreamlike and illusory, but even so, humorously you go on doing things. For example, if you are walking, without unnecessary solemnity or self-consciousness, lightheartedly walk toward the open space of truth. When you sit, be the stronghold of truth. As you eat, feed your negativities and illusions into the belly of emptiness, dissolving them into all-pervading space. And when you go to the toilet, consider all your obscurations and blockages are being cleansed and washed away.

DUDJOM RINPOCHE

May 23

It is essential to realize now, in life, when we still have a body, that its convincing appearance of solidity is a mere illusion. The most powerful way to realize this is to learn how, after meditation, to "become a child of illusion": to refrain from solidifying, as we are always tempted to do, the perceptions of ourselves and our world; and to go on, like the "child of illusion," seeing directly, as we do in meditation, that all phenomena are illusory and dreamlike. The realization that this deepens the body's illusory nature is one of the most profound and inspiring we can have to help us to let go.

When we are in a negative frame of mind, it is only natural to doubt rather than to believe.

From a Buddhist point of view, doubt is a sign of a lack of complete understanding and a lack of spiritual education, but it is also seen as a catalyst in the maturing of faith. It is when we face doubts and difficulties that we discover whether our faith is a simplistic, pious, and conceptual one, or whether it is strong, enduring, and anchored in a deep understanding in the heart.

If you have faith, sooner or later it may well be put to the test, and wherever the challenge may come from—from within you or from outside—it is simply part of the process of faith and doubt.

May 25

What can we gain by sailing to the moon if we are not able to cross the abyss that separates us from ourselves? This is the most important of all voyages of discovery, and without it, all the rest are not only useless, but disastrous.

THOMAS MERTON

May 26

Imagine you were living in a house on the top of a mountain which was itself at the top of the whole world. Suddenly the entire structure of the house, which limited your view, just falls away and you can see all around you, both outside and inside. But there is not any 'thing' to see; what happens has no ordinary reference whatsoever; it is total, complete, unprecedented, perfect seeing. This is how it feels when Rigpa is directly revealed.

May 27

Even in the greatest yogi, sorrow and joy still arise just as before. The difference between an ordinary person and the yogi is how they view their emotions and react to them.

An ordinary person will instinctively accept or reject them, and so arouse the attachment or aversion that will result in the accumulation of negative karma.

A yogi, however, perceives everything that rises in its natural, pristine state, without allowing grasping to enter his perception.

May 28

Patrul Rinpoche's teacher was called Jikmé Gyalwé
Nyugu. For many years, he had been doing a solitary
retreat in a cave in the mountains. One day when he
came outside, the sun was pouring down; he gazed out
into the sky and saw a cloud moving in the direction of
where his master, Jikmé Lingpa, lived. The thought
rose in his mind: "Over there is where my master is,"
and with that thought a tremendous feeling of longing
and devotion surged up in him. It was so strong, so
shattering, that he fainted.

When Jikmé Gyalwé Nyugu came to, the entire
blessing of his master's wisdom mind had been trans-
mitted to him, and he had reached the highest stage of
realization, what we call "the exhaustion of phenomenal reality."

May 29

In meditation, be at ease, be as natural and spacious as possible.

Slip quietly out of the noose of your habitual anxious self, release all grasping, and relax into your true nature. Think of your ordinary, emotional, thought-ridden self as a block of ice or a slab of butter left out in the sun. If you are feeling hard and cold, let this aggression melt away in the sunlight of your meditation. Let peace work on you and enable you to gather your scattered mind into the mindfulness of Calm Abiding, and awaken in you the awareness and insight of Clear Seeing. And you will find all your negativity disarmed, your aggression dissolved, and your confusion evaporating slowly like mist into the vast and stainless sky of your absolute nature.

May 30

What is born will die,
What has been gathered will be dispersed,
What has been accumulated will be exhausted,
What has been built up will collapse,
And what has been high will be brought low.

TRADITIONAL BUDDHIST SCRIPTURE

May 31

How can we work to overcome attachment? Only by realizing its impermanent nature; this realization slowly releases us from its grip. We come to glimpse what the masters say the true attitude to change can be: as if we were the sky looking at the clouds passing by, or as free as mercury. When mercury is dropped on the ground, its very nature is to remain intact; it never mixes with the dust.

As we try to follow the masters' advice and are slowly released from attachment, a great compassion is released in us. The clouds of grasping part and disperse, and the sun of our true compassionate heart shines out.

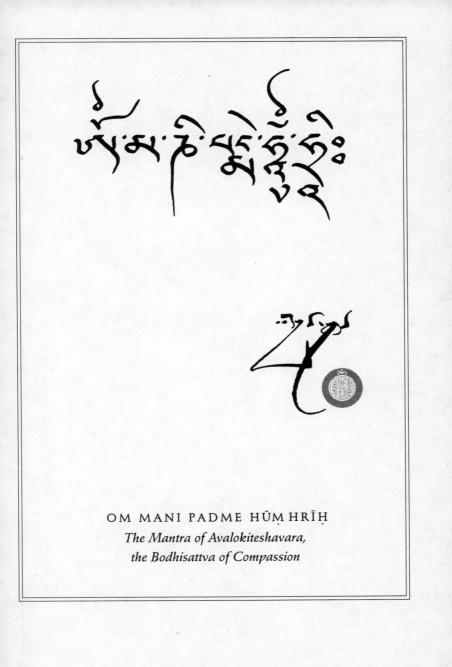

OM MANI PADME HŪM HRĪḤ
The Mantra of Avalokiteshavara,
the Bodhisattva of Compassion

June 1

Quietly sitting, body still, speech silent, mind at peace, let thoughts and emotions, whatever rises, come and go, without clinging to anything.

What does this state feel like? Dudjom Rinpoche used to say: Imagine a man who comes home after a long, hard day's work in the fields, and sinks into his favorite chair in front of the fire. He has been working all day and he knows that he has achieved what he wanted to achieve; there is nothing more to worry about, nothing left unaccomplished, and he can let go completely of all his cares and concerns, content, simply, to be.

June 2

If your mind is empty, it is always ready for anything; it is open to everything. In the beginner's mind there are many possibilities, in the expert's mind there are few.

SUZUKI-ROSHI

June 3

Devotion is the essence of the path, and if we have in mind nothing but the guru and feel nothing but fervent devotion, whatever occurs is perceived as his blessing. If we simply practice with this constantly present devotion, this is prayer itself.

When all thoughts are imbued with devotion to the guru, there is a natural confidence that this will take care of whatever may happen. All forms are the guru, all sounds are prayer, and all gross and subtle thoughts arise as devotion. Everything is spontaneously liberated in the absolute nature, like knots untied in the sky.

DILGO KHYENTSE RINPOCHE

What is compassion? It is not simply a sense of sympathy or caring for the person suffering, not simply a warmth of heart toward the person before you, or a sharp clarity of recognition of their needs and pain, it is also a sustained and practical determination to do whatever is possible and necessary to help alleviate their suffering.

June 5

As you continue to practice meditation, you may have all kinds of *experiences,* both good and bad. You might experience states of bliss, clarity, or absence of thoughts. In one way these are very good experiences, and signs of progress in meditation. For when you experience *bliss,* it's a sign that *desire* has temporarily dissolved. When you experience real *clarity,* it's a sign that *aggression* has temporarily ceased. When you experience a state of *absence of thought,* it's a sign that your *ignorance* has temporarily died. By themselves they are good experiences, but if you get attached to them, they become obstacles.

Experiences are not realization in themselves; but if we remain free of attachment to them, they become what they really are—that is, *materials for realization.*

June 6

Looking into death needn't be frightening or morbid. Why not reflect on death when you are really inspired, relaxed, and comfortable, lying in bed, or on vacation, or listening to music that particularly delights you? Why not reflect on it when you are happy, in good health, confident, and full of well-being? Don't you notice that there are particular moments when you are naturally inspired to introspection? Work with them gently, for *these are the moments when you can go through a powerful experience, and your whole worldview can change quickly.* These are the moments when former beliefs crumble on their own, and you can find yourself being transformed.

June 7

In my tradition of meditation, your eyes should be kept open: This is a very important point. If you are sensitive to disturbances from outside, when you begin to practice you may find it helpful to close your eyes for a while and quietly go within.

Once you feel established in calm, gradually open your eyes, and you will find that your gaze has grown more peaceful and tranquil. Now look down, along the line of your nose, at an angle of about 45 degrees in front of you. One practical tip in general is that whenever your mind is wild, it is best to lower your gaze, and whenever it is dull and sleepy, to bring your gaze up.

Once your mind is calm and the clarity of insight begins to arise, you will feel free to bring your gaze up, opening your eyes more and looking into the space directly in front of you. This is the gaze recommended in the Dzogchen practice.

June 8

I am never far from those with faith, or even from those without it, though they do not see me. My children will always, always, be protected by my compassion.

PADMASAMBHAVA

June 9

If we are interdependent with everything and everyone, even our smallest, least significant thought, word, and action have real consequences throughout the universe.

Throw a pebble into a pond. It sends a shiver across the surface of the water. Ripples merge into one another and create new ones. Everything is inextricably interrelated: We come to realize that we are responsible for everything we do, say, or think, responsible in fact for ourselves, everyone and everything else, and the entire universe.

June 10

———————

Take care not to impose anything on the mind. When you meditate, there should be no effort to control, and no attempt to be peaceful. Don't be overly solemn or feel that you are taking part in some special ritual; let go even of the idea that you are meditating. Let your body remain as it is, and your breath as you find it.

Think of yourself as the sky, holding the whole universe.

June 11

Buddha recognized that ignorance of our true nature is the root of all the torment of samsara, and the root of ignorance itself is the mind's habitual tendency to distraction.

To end the mind's distraction would be to end samsara itself; the key to this, he realized, is to *bring the mind home* to its true nature, through the practice of meditation.

June 12

There would be no chance at all of getting to know death if it happened only once. But fortunately, life is nothing but a continuing dance of birth and death, a dance of change. Every time I hear the rush of a mountain stream, or the waves crashing on the shore, or my own heartbeat, I hear the sound of impermanence. These changes, these small deaths, are our living links with death. They are death's pulses, death's heartbeat, prompting us to let go of all the things we cling to.

Sit for a short time; then take a break, a very short break of about thirty seconds or a minute. But be mindful of whatever you do, and do not lose your presence and its natural ease. Then alert yourself and sit again. If you do many short sessions like this, your breaks will often make your meditation more real and more inspiring; they will take the clumsy, irksome rigidity, solemnity, and unnaturalness out of your practice and bring you more and more focus and ease. Gradually, through this interplay of breaks and sitting, the barrier between meditation and everyday life will crumble, the contrast between them will dissolve, and you will find yourself increasingly in your natural pure presence, without distraction.

Then, as Dudjom Rinpoche used to say: "Even though the meditator may leave the meditation, the meditation will not leave the meditator."

June 14

Because the law of karma is inevitable and infallible, whenever we harm others, we are directly harming ourselves, and whenever we bring them happiness, we are bringing ourselves future happiness. The Dalai Lama says:

"If you try to subdue your selfish motives—anger and so forth—and develop more kindness and compassion for others, ultimately you yourself will benefit more than you would otherwise. So sometimes I say that the wise selfish person should practice this way. Foolish selfish people are always thinking of themselves, and the result is negative. Wise selfish people think of others, help others as much as they can, and the result is that they too receive benefit."

June 15

The teachings of all the great mystical paths of the world make it clear that there is within us an enormous reservoir of power, the power of wisdom and compassion, the power of what Christ called the Kingdom of Heaven. If we learn how to use it—and this is the goal of the search for enlightenment—it can transform not only ourselves but the world around us. Has there ever been a time when the clear use of this sacred power was more essential or more urgent? Has there ever been a time when it was more vital to understand the nature of this pure power and how to channel it and how to use it for the sake of the world?

June 16

Sometimes I tease people and ask: "What makes you so adamant that there's no life after death? What proof do *you* have? What if you found there was a life after this one, having died denying its existence?"

Those of us who undertake a spiritual discipline—of meditation, for example—come to discover many things about our own minds that we did not know before. For as our minds open more and more to the extraordinary, vast, and hitherto unsuspected existence of the nature of mind, we begin to glimpse a completely different dimension, one in which all of our assumptions about our identity and reality, which we thought we knew so well, start to dissolve, and in which the possibility of lives other than this one becomes at least likely. We begin to understand that everything we are being told by the masters about life and death, and life after death, is real.

June 17

There could be no bigger mistake than to think that ignorance is somehow dumb and stupid, or passive and lacking in intelligence. On the contrary, it is shrewd and cunning, versatile and ingenious in the games of deception, and in our wrong views and their burning convictions we find one of its deepest and, as Buddha said, most dangerous manifestations:

> *What do you have to fear from the wild elephant*
> *Who can only damage your body here and now,*
> *When falling under the influence of misguided people*
>   *and wrong views*
> *Not only destroys the merit you have accumulated in the*
>   *past,*
> *But also blocks your path to freedom in the future?*

June 18

Since pure awareness of nowness is the real buddha,
In openness and contentment I found the Lama in my
*   heart.*
When we realize this unending natural mind is the very
*   nature of the Lama,*
Then there is no need for attached, grasping , or
*   weeping prayers or artificial complaints,*
By simply relaxing in this uncontrived, open, and
*   natural state,*
We obtain the blessing of aimless self-liberation of
*   whatever arises.*

DUDJOM RINPOCHE

June 19

Whatever you do, don't shut off your pain; accept your pain and remain vulnerable. However desperate you become, accept your pain as it is, because it is in fact trying to hand you a priceless gift: the chance of discovering, through spiritual practice, what lies behind sorrow.

"Grief," Rumi wrote, "can be the garden of compassion. If you keep your heart open through everything, your pain can become your greatest ally in your life's search for love and wisdom."

June 20

When you have fully recognized that the nature of your mind is the same as that of the master, from then on you and the master can never be separate, because the master is *one* with the nature of your mind, always present, as it is.

When you have recognized that the master and you are inseparable, an enormous gratitude and sense of awe and homage is born in you. Dudjom Rinpoche calls this "the homage of the View." It is a devotion that springs spontaneously from seeing the View of the nature of mind.

Imagine vividly a situation where you have acted badly, one about which you feel guilty, and about which you wince even to think of it.

Then, as you breathe in, accept total responsibility for your actions in that particular situation, without in any way trying to justify your behavior. Acknowledge exactly what you have done wrong, and wholeheartedly ask for forgiveness. Now, as you breathe out, send out reconciliation, forgiveness, healing, and understanding.

So you breathe in blame, and breathe out the undoing of harm; you breathe in responsibility, breathe out healing, forgiveness, and reconciliation.

This exercise is particularly powerful and may give you the courage to go to see the person whom you have wronged, and the strength and willingness to talk to him or her directly and actually ask for forgiveness from the depths of your heart.

June 22

What really matters is not just the practice of sitting but far more the state of mind you find yourself in after meditation. It is this calm and centered state of mind you should prolong through everything you do. I like the Zen story in which the disciple asked his master:

"Master, how do you put enlightenment into action? How do you practice it in everyday life?"

"By eating and by sleeping," replied the master.

"But Master, everybody sleeps and everybody eats."

"But not everybody eats when they eat, and not everybody sleeps when they sleep."

From this comes the famous Zen saying, "When I eat, I eat; when I sleep, I sleep."

To eat when you eat and sleep when you sleep means to be completely present in all your actions, with none of the distractions of ego to stop you from being there. This is integration.

June 23

Think of the moment of death as a strange border zone of the mind, a no-man's land in which, on one hand, if we do not understand the illusory nature of our body, we might suffer vast emotional trauma as we lose it, and on the other we are presented with the possibility of limitless freedom, a freedom that springs precisely from the absence of that very same body.

When we are at last freed from the body that has defined and dominated our understanding of ourselves for so long, the karmic vision of one life is completely exhausted, but any karma that might be created in the future has not yet begun to crystallize.

So what happens in death is that there is a "gap," or space, that is fertile with vast possibility; it is a moment of tremendous, pregnant power where the only thing that matters, or could matter, is how exactly the mind is. Stripped of a physical body, the mind stands naked, revealed startlingly for what it has always been: the architect of our reality.

June 24

I remember how people would often come to see my master Jamyang Khyentse simply to ask for his guidance for the moment of death. He was so loved and revered throughout Tibet, especially in the eastern province of Kham, that some would travel for months on end to meet him and get his blessing just once before they died. All my masters would give this as their advice, for this is the essence of what is needed as you come to die:

"Be free of attachment and aversion. Keep your mind pure. And unite your mind with Buddha."

He who binds to himself a Joy,
Does the winged life destroy;
He who kisses the Joy as it flies,
Lives in Eternity's sunrise.

WILLIAM BLAKE

June 26

When you arrive naturally at a state of meditation, inspired by the View, you can remain there for a long time without any distraction or special effort. There is nothing called "meditation" to protect or sustain, for you are in the natural flow of the wisdom of Rigpa. And you realize, when you are in it, that is how it has always been, and is. When the wisdom of Rigpa shines, not one shadow of doubt can remain, and a deep, complete understanding arises, effortlessly and directly.

This moment is the moment of awakening. A profound sense of humor wells up from within, and you smile in amusement at how inadequate were all your former concepts and ideas about the nature of mind.

June 27

There are several reasons for keeping your eyes open when you practice meditation. With your eyes open, you are less likely to fall asleep. Then, meditation is not a means of running away from the world, or of escaping from it into a trancelike experience of an altered state of consciousness. On the contrary, it is a direct way to help us truly understand ourselves and to relate to life and the world.

Therefore, in meditation you keep your eyes open, not closed. Instead of shutting out life, you remain open and at peace with everything. You leave all your senses—hearing, seeing, feeling—just open, naturally, as they are, without grasping after their perceptions.

Whatever you see, whatever you hear, leave it as it is, without grasping. Leave the hearing in the hearing, leave the seeing in the seeing, without letting your attachment enter into the perception.

June 28

Reflect on this: The realization of impermanence is paradoxically the only thing we can hold on to, perhaps our only lasting possession. It is like the sky, or the earth. No matter how much everything around us may change or collapse, they endure.

Say we go through a shattering emotional crisis . . . our whole life seems to be disintegrating . . . our husband or wife suddenly leaves us without warning. The earth is still there; the sky is still there. Of course, even the earth trembles now and again, just to remind us that we cannot take anything for granted. . . .

June 29

All the Buddhist teachings are explained in terms of Ground, Path, and Fruition. The ground of Dzogchen is the fundamental, primordial state, our absolute nature, which is already perfect and always present.

Patrul Rinpoche says: "It is neither to be sought externally, nor is it something you did not have before and that now has to be newly born in your mind." So from the point of view of the Ground—the absolute— our nature is the same as the buddhas', and there is no question at this level, "not a hair's breadth," the masters say, of teaching or practice to do.

June 30

The Dzogchen masters are acutely aware of the dangers of confusing the absolute with the relative. People who fail to understand this relationship can overlook and even disdain the relative aspects of spiritual practice and the karmic law of cause and effect. However, those who truly seize the meaning of Dzogchen will have only a deeper respect for karma, as well as a keener and more urgent appreciation of the need for purification and for spiritual practice. This is because they will understand the vastness of what it is in them that has been obscured, and so endeavor all the more fervently, and with an always fresh, natural discipline, to remove whatever stands between them and their true nature.

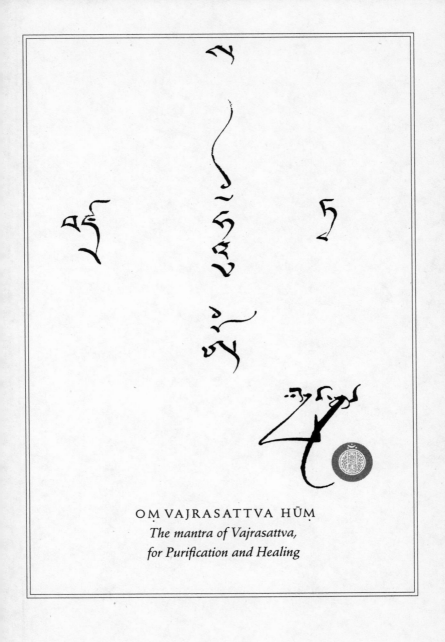

OṂ VAJRASATTVA HŪṂ

*The mantra of Vajrasattva,
for Purification and Healing*

In meditation, negative experiences are the most misleading, because we tend to take them as a bad sign. But in fact the negative experiences in our practice are blessings in disguise. Try to not react to them with aversion as you might normally do, but recognize them instead for what they truly are, merely experiences, illusory and dreamlike.

The realization of the true nature of the experience liberates you from the harm or danger of the experience itself, and as a result a negative experience can become a source of great blessing and accomplishment. There are innumerable stories of how masters worked like this with negative experiences and transformed them into catalysts for realization.

July 2

We often wonder what to do about negativity or certain troubling emotions. In the spaciousness of meditation, you can view your thoughts and emotions with a totally unbiased attitude. When your attitude changes, then the whole atmosphere of your mind changes, even the very nature of your thoughts and emotions. When *you* become more agreeable, then *they* do; if *you* have no difficulty with them, *they* will have no difficulty with you either.

July 3

Imagine that you are having difficulties with a loved one, such as your mother or father, husband or wife, lover or friend. How helpful and revealing it can be to consider the other person not in his or her "role" of mother or father or husband, but simply as another "you," another human being, with the same feelings as you, the same desire for happiness, the same fear of suffering. Thinking of the other one as a real person, exactly the same as you, will open your heart to him or her and give you more insight into how to help.

July 4

In meditation, as in all arts, there has to be a delicate balance between relaxation and alertness. Once a monk called Shrona was studying meditation with one of Buddha's closest disciples. He had difficulty finding the right frame of mind. He tried very hard to concentrate, and gave himself a headache. Then he relaxed his mind, but so much that he fell asleep. Finally he appealed to Buddha for help.

Knowing that Shrona had been a famous musician before he became a monk, Buddha asked him: "Weren't you a *vina* player when you were a layperson?"

Shrona nodded.

"How did you get the best sound out of your *vina*? Was it when the strings were very tight or when they were very loose?"

"Neither. When they had just the right tension, neither too taut nor too slack."

"Well, it's exactly the same with your mind."

July 5

In horror of death, I took to the mountains—
Again and again I meditated on the uncertainty of the
  hour of death,
Capturing the fortress of the deathless unending nature
  of mind.
Now all fear of death is over and done.

MILAREPA

July 6

The teachings tell us what it is we need to realize, but we also have to go on our own journey, in order to come to a personal realization. That journey may take us through suffering, difficulties, and doubts of all kinds, but they will become our greatest teachers. Through them we will learn the humility to recognize our limitations, and through them we will discover the inner strength and fearlessness we need to emerge from our old habits and set patterns, and surrender into the vaster vision of real freedom offered by the spiritual teachings.

July 7

We are so addicted to looking outside ourselves that we have lost access to our inner being almost completely. We are terrified to look inward, because our culture has given us no idea of what we will find. We may even think that if we do, we will be in danger of madness. This is one of the last and most resourceful ploys of ego to prevent us from discovering our real nature.

So we make our lives so hectic that we eliminate the slightest risk of looking into ourselves. Even the idea of meditation can scare people. When they hear the words *egoless* or *emptiness,* they think that experiencing those states will be like being thrown out the door of a spaceship to float forever in a dark, chilling void. Nothing could be further from the truth. But in a world dedicated to distraction, silence and stillness terrify us; we protect ourselves from them with noise and frantic busyness. Looking into the nature of our mind is the last thing we would dare to do.

July 8

Profound and tranquil, free from complexity,
Uncompounded luminous clarity,
Beyond the mind of conceptual ideas;
This is the depth of the mind of the Victorious Ones.

In this there is not a thing to be removed,
Nor anything that needs to be added.
It is merely the immaculate
Looking naturally at itself.

NYOSHUH KHEN RINPOCHE

July 9

In today's highly interdependent world, individuals and nations can no longer resolve many of their problems by themselves. We need one another. We must therefore develop a sense of universal responsibility. . . . It is our collective and individual responsibility to protect and nurture the global family, to support its weaker members, and to preserve and tend to the environment in which we all live.

THE DALAI LAMA

Difficulties and obstacles, if properly understood and used, can turn out to be an unexpected source of strength. Gesar was the great warrior king of Tibet, whose escapades form the greatest epic of Tibetan literature. *Gesar* means "indomitable," someone who can never be put down. From the moment Gesar was born, his evil uncle Trotung tried all kinds of means to kill him. But with each attempt Gesar only grew stronger and stronger.

For the Tibetans, Gesar is not only a martial warrior but also a spiritual one. To be a spiritual warrior means to develop a special kind of courage, one that is innately intelligent, gentle, and fearless. Spiritual warriors can still be frightened, but even so they are courageous enough to taste suffering, to relate clearly to their fundamental fear, and to draw out without evasion the lessons from difficulties.

A direct reflection on what death means and the many facets of the truth of impermanence can enable us to make rich use of this life while we still have time, and ensure that when we die it will be without remorse or self-recrimination at having wasted our lives.

As Tibet's famous poet-saint, Milarepa, said: "My religion is to live—and die—without regret."

July 12

With mind far off, not thinking of death's coming,
Performing these meaningless activities,
Returning empty-handed now would be complete
    confusion;
The need is recognition, the spiritual teachings,
So why not practice the path of wisdom at this very
    moment?
From the mouths of the saints come these words:
If you do not keep your master's teaching in your heart
Will you not become your own deceiver?

THE TIBETAN BOOK OF THE DEAD

July 13

"Training" the mind does not in any way mean forcibly subjugating or brainwashing the mind. To train the mind is first to see directly and concretely how the mind functions, a knowledge that you derive from spiritual teachings and through personal experience in meditation practice. Then you use that understanding to tame the mind and work with it skillfully, to make it more and more pliable, so that you can become master of your mind and employ it to its fullest and most beneficial end.

To serve the world out of the dynamic union of wisdom and compassion would be to participate most effectively in the preservation of the planet. Masters of all the religious traditions on earth now understand that spiritual training is *essential* not solely for monks and nuns but for all people, whatever their faith or way of life. The nature of spiritual development is intensely practical, active, and effective. The danger we are all in together makes it essential now that we no longer think of spiritual development as a luxury but as a necessity for survival.

As a famous Tibetan teaching says: "When the world is filled with evil, all mishaps should be transformed into the path of enlightenment."

July 15

The basis on which Buddhist[s] accept the concept of rebirth is principally the continuity of consciousness. . . . If you trace our present mind or consciousness back, then you will find that you are tracing the origin of the continuity of mind into an infinite dimension; it is, as you will see, beginningless.

Therefore there must be successive rebirths that allow that continuum of mind to be there.

THE DALAI LAMA

July 16

Two people have been living in you all your life. One is the ego, garrulous, demanding, hysterical, calculating; the other is the hidden spiritual being, whose still voice of wisdom you have only rarely heard or attended to. As you listen more and more to the teachings, contemplate them, and integrate them into your life, your inner voice, your innate wisdom of discernment, what we call in Buddhism "discriminating awareness," is awakened and strengthened, and you begin to distinguish between its guidance and the various clamorous and enthralling voices of ego. The memory of your real nature, with all its splendor and confidence, begins to return to you.

You will find, in fact, that you have uncovered in yourself your own *wise guide*, and as the voice of your wise guide, or discriminating awareness, grows stronger and clearer, you will start to distinguish between its truth and the various deceptions of the ego, and you will be able to listen to it with discernment and confidence.

July 17

The root of all phenomena is your mind.
If unexamined, it rushes after experiences, ingenious in
  the games of deception.
If you look right into it, it is free of any ground or origin,
In essence free of any coming, staying or going.

JAMYANG KHYENTSE CHÖKYI LODRÖ

July 18

Don't we know, only too well, that protection from pain doesn't work, and that when we try to defend ourselves from suffering, we only suffer more and don't learn what we can from the experience? As Rilke wrote, the protected heart that is "never exposed to loss, innocent and secure, cannot know tenderness; only the won-back heart can ever be satisfied: free, through all it has given up, to rejoice in its mastery."

July 19

All we need to do to receive direct help is to ask. Didn't Christ also say: "Ask, and it shall be given you; seek and ye shall find; knock and it shall be opened unto you. Everyone that asketh receiveth; and he that seeketh findeth"? And yet asking is what we find hardest. Many of us, I feel, hardly know *how* to ask. Sometimes it is because we are arrogant, sometimes because we are unwilling to seek help, sometimes because we are lazy, and sometimes because our minds are so busy with questions, distractions, and confusion that the simplicity of asking does not occur to us.

The turning point in any healing of alcoholics or drug addicts is when they admit their illness and ask for aid. In one way or another, we are all addicts of samsara; the moment when help can come for us is when we admit our addiction and simply ask.

Imagine that you had gone all your life without ever washing, and then one day you decide to take a shower. You start scrubbing away, but then watch in horror as the dirt begins to ooze out of the pores of your skin and stream down your body. Something must be wrong: You were supposed to be getting cleaner and all you can see is grime. You panic and fling yourself out of the shower, convinced that you should never have begun. But you only end up even more dirty than before. You have no way of knowing that the wisest thing to do is to be patient and to finish the shower. It may look for a while as if you are getting even dirtier, but if you keep on washing, you will emerge fresh and clean. It's all a process, the process of purification.

Whenever doubt arises, see it simply as an obstacle, recognize it as an understanding that is calling out to be clarified or unblocked, and know that it is not a fundamental problem but simply a stage in the process of purification and learning. Allow the process to continue and complete itself, and never lose your trust or resolve. This is the way followed by all the great practitioners of the past, who used to say: "There is no armor like perseverance."

July 21

If, at the moment of death, you can unite your mind confidently with the wisdom mind of the master and die in that peace, then all, I promise and assure you, will be well.

Our task in life is to practice this merging with the wisdom mind of the master again and again, so that it becomes so natural that every activity—sitting, walking, eating, drinking, sleeping, dreaming and waking—starts to be increasingly permeated by the master's living presence. Slowly, over years of focused devotion, you begin to know and realize all appearances to be the display of the wisdom of the master. All the situations of life, even those that once seemed tragic, meaningless, or terrifying, reveal themselves more and more transparently to be the direct teaching and blessing of the master, and the inner teacher.

July 22

There are many ways of making the approach to meditation as joyful as possible. You can find the music that most exalts you and use it to open your heart and mind. You can collect pieces of poetry, or quotations or lines of teachings that over the years have moved you, and keep them always at hand to elevate your spirit. I have always loved Tibetan *thangka* paintings and derive strength from their beauty. You too can find reproductions of paintings that arouse a sense of sacredness, and hang them on the walls of your room.

Listen to a cassette tape of a teaching by a great master, or a sacred chant. You can make of the place where you meditate a simple paradise, with one flower, one stick of incense, one candle, one photograph of an enlightened master, or one statue of a deity or a buddha. You can transform the most ordinary of rooms into an intimate sacred space, an environment where every day you go to meet with your true self with all the joy and happy ceremony of one old friend greeting another.

July 23

From the blossoming lotus of devotion, at the center of
   my heart,
Rise up, O compassionate master, my only refuge!
I am plagued by past actions and turbulent emotions:
To protect me in my misfortune
Remain as the jewel-ornament on the crown of my
   head, the mandala of great bliss,
Arousing all my mindfulness and awareness, I pray!

JIKMÉ LINGPA

July 24

The masters tell us that there is an aspect of our minds that is its fundamental basis, a state called "the ground of the ordinary mind." It functions like a storehouse, in which the imprints of past actions caused by our negative emotions are all stored like seeds. When the right conditions arise, they germinate and manifest as circumstances and situations in our lives.

If we have a habit of thinking in a particular pattern, positive or negative, then these tendencies will be triggered and provoked very easily, and recur and go on recurring. With constant repetition our inclinations and habits become steadily more entrenched, and continue, increasing and gathering power, even when we sleep. This is how they come to determine our life, our death, and our rebirth.

July 25

When the wisdom of Rigpa shines, a growing sense of tremendous and unshakable certainty and conviction that "this is it" rises up: There is nothing further to seek, nothing more that could possibly be hoped for. This certainty of the View is what has to be deepened through glimpse after glimpse of the nature of mind, and stabilized through the continuous discipline of meditation.

July 26

Dzogchen meditation is subtly powerful in dealing with the arisings of the mind and has a unique perspective on them. All the risings are seen in their true nature, not as separate from Rigpa, and not as antagonistic to it, but actually as none other—and this is very important—than its "self-radiance," the manifestation of its very energy.

July 27

Who is the outer teacher? None other than the embodiment and voice and representative of our inner teacher. The master whose human shape and human voice and wisdom we come to love with a love deeper than any other in our lives is none other than the external manifestation of the mystery of our own inner truth. What else could explain why we feel so strongly connected to him or her?

July 28

Though different forms are perceived, they are in essence empty; yet in the emptiness one perceives forms.

Though different sounds are heard, they are empty; yet in the emptiness one perceives sounds.

Also different thoughts arise; they are empty, yet in the emptiness one perceives thoughts.

DUDJOM RINPOCHE

July 29

For Tibetans, the main festival of the year is the New Year, which is like Christmas, Easter, Thanksgiving and your birthday all rolled into one. Patrul Rinpoche was a great master whose life was full of eccentric episodes that would bring the teaching to life. Instead of celebrating New Year's Day and wishing people a "Happy New Year" like everyone else, Patrul Rinpoche used to weep. When asked why, he said that another year had gone by, and so many people had come one year closer to death, *still unprepared*.

July 30

If, at the moment of death, we have already a stable realization of the nature of mind, in one instant we can purify all our karma. And if we continue that stable recognition, we will actually be able to end our karma altogether, by entering the expanse of the primordial purity of the nature of mind, and attaining liberation.

Padmasambhava explained this: "This power to attain stability by just recognizing the nature of mind is like a torch which in one instant can clear away the darkness of aeons. *So if we can recognize the nature of mind in the bardo in the same way as we can now when it is introduced by the master, there is not the slightest doubt that we will attain enlightenment. This is why, from this very moment on, we must become familiar with the nature of mind through practice.*"

July 31

When you meditate, it is essential to create the right inner environment of the mind. All effort and struggle come from not being spacious, and so creating that right environment is vital for your meditation truly to happen.

When humor and spaciousness *are* present, meditation arises effortlessly.

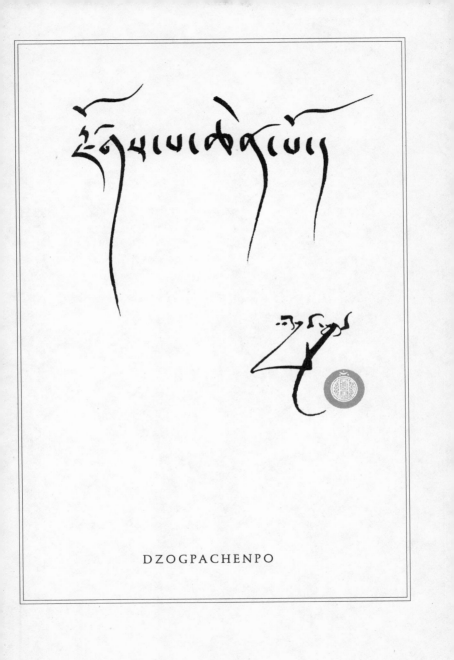

DZOGPACHENPO

One of the most important revelations of the near-death experience is how it transforms the lives of those who have been through it. One man said:

"I was transformed from a man who was lost and wandering aimlessly, with no goal in life other than a desire for material wealth, to someone who had a deep motivation, a purpose in life, a definite direction, and an overpowering conviction that there would be a reward at the end of life. My interest in material wealth and greed for possessions were replaced by a thirst for spiritual understanding and a passionate desire to see world conditions improve."

August 2

How sad it is that most of us only begin to appreciate our lives when we are on the point of dying. I often think of the words of the great Buddhist master Padmasambhava: "Those who believe they have plenty of time get ready only at the time of death. Then they are ravaged by regret. But isn't it far too late?"

August 3

When the sun of fierce devotion shines on the snow mountain of the master, the stream of his blessing will pour down.

The Tibetan Saint, DRIKUNG KYOBPA

For all its dangers, today's world is also a very exciting one. The modern mind is slowly opening to different visions of reality. Great teachers like the Dalai Lama and Mother Teresa can be seen on television; many masters from the East now visit and teach in the West; and books from all the mystical traditions are winning an increasingly large audience. The desperate situation of the planet is slowly waking people up to the necessity for transformation on a global scale.

Enlightenment is real, and there are enlightened masters still on the earth. When you actually meet one, you will be shaken and moved in the depths of your heart and you will realize that all the words, such as *illumination* and *wisdom,* that you thought were only ideas are in fact true.

August 5

Considering others to be *just the same as yourself* helps you to open up your relationships and give them a new and richer meaning. Imagine if societies and nations began to view one another in the same way; at last we would have the beginnings of a solid basis for peace on earth, and the happy coexistence of all peoples.

August 6

"In meditation practice, you might experience a muddy, semiconscious, drifting state, like having a hood over your head: a dreamy dullness. This is really nothing more than a kind of blurred and mindless stagnation. How do you get out of this state? Alert yourself, straighten your back, breathe the stale air out of your lungs, and direct your awareness into clear space to freshen your mind. If you remain in this stagnant state you will not evolve, so whenever this setback arises, clear it again and again. It is important to be as watchful as possible, and to stay as vigilant as you can."

DUDJOM RINPOCHE

The moment of death is a tremendous opportunity, if we understand clearly what is happening and have prepared well for it in life. For at the actual moment of death, the thinking ego-mind dies into the essence, and in this truth, enlightenment takes place. If we familiarize ourselves with the true nature of mind through practice while we are alive, we become more prepared for when it reveals itself spontaneously at the moment of death. Recognition then follows as naturally as a child running into its mother's lap. Remaining in that state, we are liberated.

August 8

Sentient beings are as limitless as the whole of space:
May they each effortlessly realize the nature of their
mind,
And may every single being of all the six realms, who
has each been in one life or another my father or
mother,
Attain all together the ground of primordial perfection.

August 9

What most of us need, almost more than anything, is the courage and humility really to ask for help, from the depths of our hearts: to ask for the compassion of the enlightened beings, to ask for purification and healing, to ask for the power to understand the meaning of our suffering and transform it; at a *relative* level to ask for the growth in our lives of clarity, peace, and discernment, and to ask for the realization of the *absolute* nature of mind that comes from merging with the deathless wisdom mind of the master.

August 10

This existence of ours is as transient as autumn clouds
To watch the birth and death of beings is like looking at
   the movements of a dance.
A lifetime is like a flash of lightning in the sky,
Rushing by, like a torrent down a steep mountain.

BUDDHA

August 11

To work with changes now, in life: That is the real way to prepare for death. Life may be full of pain, suffering, and difficulty, but all of these are opportunities handed to us to help us move toward an emotional acceptance of death. It is only when we believe things to be permanent that we shut off the possibility of learning from change.

August 12

My master had a student called Apa Pant, a distinguished Indian diplomat and author, who served as Indian ambassador in a number of capital cities around the world. He was also a practitioner of meditation and yoga, and each time he saw my master, he would always ask him "how to meditate." He was following an Eastern tradition where the student keeps asking the master one simple, basic question over and over again.

One day when our master Jamyang Khyentse was watching a Lama Dance in front of the Palace Temple in Gangtok, the capital of Sikkim, he was chuckling at the antics of the *atsara,* the clown who provides light relief between dances. Apa Pant kept pestering him, asking him again and again how to meditate, so this time when my master replied, it was in such a way as to let him know that he was telling him once and for all: "Look, it's like this: When the past thought has ceased, and the future thought has not yet risen, isn't there a gap?"

"Yes," said Apa Pant.

"Well, prolong it: That is meditation."

August 13

The most compassionate insight of my tradition and its noblest contribution to the spiritual wisdom of humanity has been its understanding and repeated enactment of the ideal of the bodhisattva, the being who takes on the suffering of all sentient beings, who undertakes the journey to liberation not for his or her own good alone but to help all others, and who eventually, after attaining liberation, does not dissolve into the absolute or flee the agony of samsara, but chooses to return again and again to devote his or her wisdom and compassion to the service of the whole world.

August 14

One of the greatest of Tibet's many woman masters, Ma Chik Lap Drön, said: "Alert, alert; yet relax, relax. This is a crucial point for the View in meditation."

Alert your alertness, but at the same time be relaxed, so relaxed in fact that you don't even hold on to an idea of relaxation.

August 15

The successive existences in a series of rebirths are not like the pearls in a pearl necklace, held together by a string, the 'soul,' which passes through all the pearls; rather they are like dice piled one on top of the other. Each die is separate, but it supports the one above it, with which it is functionally connected. Between the dice there is no identity, but conditionality.

H. W. SCHUMANN
THE HISTORICAL BUDDHA

August 16

The more often you listen to your discriminating awareness, the more easily you will be able to change your negative moods yourself, see through them, and even laugh at them for the absurd dramas and ridiculous illusions that they are.

Gradually you will find yourself able to free yourself more and more quickly from the dark emotions that have ruled your life, and this ability to do so is the greatest miracle of all.

The Tibetan mystic, Tertön Sogyal, said that he was not really impressed by someone who could turn the floor into the ceiling or fire into water. A real miracle, he said, was if someone could liberate just one negative emotion.

Bereavement can force you to look at your life directly, compelling you to find a purpose in it where there may not have been one before. When suddenly you find yourself alone after the death of someone you love, it can feel as if you are being given a new life and are being asked: "What will you do with this life? And why do you wish to continue living?"

My heartfelt advice to those in the depths of grief and despair after losing someone they dearly loved is to pray for help and strength and grace. Pray that you will survive and discover the richest possible meaning to the new life you now find yourself in. Be vulnerable and receptive, be courageous and patient. Above all, look into your life to find ways of sharing your love more deeply with others now.

August 18

Planning for the future is like going fishing in a dry
  gulch;
Nothing ever works out as you wanted, so give up all
  your schemes and ambitions.
If you have got to think about something—
Make it the uncertainty of the hour of your death.

GYALSÉ RINPOCHE

August 19

Again and again we need to appreciate the subtle workings of the teachings and the practice, and even when there is no extraordinary, dramatic change, to persevere with calm and patience. How important it is to be skillful and gentle with ourselves, without becoming disheartened or giving up, but trusting the spiritual path and knowing that it has its own laws and its own dynamics.

At every moment in our lives we need compassion, but what more urgent moment could there be than when we are dying? What more wonderful and consoling gift could you give to dying people than the knowledge that they are being prayed for, and that you are taking on their suffering and purifying their negative karma through your practice for them?

Even if they don't know that you are practicing for them, you are helping them and in turn they are helping you. They are actively helping you to develop your compassion, and so to purify and heal yourself. For me, all dying people are teachers, giving to all those who help them a chance to transform themselves through developing their compassion.

August 21

When you meditate, keep your mouth slightly open as if about to say a deep, relaxing "Aaah." By keeping the mouth slightly open and breathing mainly through the mouth, it is said that the "karmic winds" that create discursive thoughts are normally less likely to arise and create obstacles in your mind and meditation.

Do not make the mistake of imagining that the nature of mind is exclusive only to our minds. It is in fact the nature of everything. It can never be said too often that to realize the nature of mind is to realize the nature of all things.

August 23

If you find that meditation does not come easily in your city room, be inventive and go out into nature. Nature is always an unfailing fountain of inspiration. To calm your mind, go for a walk at dawn in the park, or watch the dew on a rose in a garden. Lie on the ground and gaze up into the sky, and let your mind expand into its spaciousness. Let the sky outside awaken a sky inside your mind. Stand by a stream and mingle your mind with its rushing; become one with its ceaseless sound. Sit by a waterfall and let its healing laughter purify your spirit. Walk on a beach and take the sea wind full and sweet against your face. Celebrate and use the beauty of moonlight to poise your mind. Sit by a lake or in a garden and, breathing quietly, let your mind fall silent as the moon comes up majestically and slowly in the cloudless night.

August 24

In death all the components of the body and mind are stripped away and disintegrate. As the body dies, the senses and subtle elements dissolve, and this is followed by the death of the ordinary aspect of the mind, with all its negative emotions of anger, desire, and ignorance. Finally nothing remains to obscure our true nature, as everything that in life has clouded the enlightened mind has fallen away. And what is revealed is the primordial ground of our absolute nature, which is like a pure and cloudless sky.

This is called the dawning of the Ground Luminosity, or Clear Light, where consciousness itself dissolves into the all-encompassing space of truth. *The Tibetan Book of the Dead* says of this moment:

> *The nature of everything is open, empty and naked like the sky.*
> *Luminous emptiness, without center or circumference; the pure, naked Rigpa dawns.*

August 25

These teachings on the bardos come from the wisdom mind of the buddhas, who can see life and death like looking in the palms of their hands.

We too are buddhas. So if we can practice in the bardo of this life, and go deeper and deeper into the nature of our mind, then we can discover this knowledge of the bardos, and the truth of these teachings will unfold in us by itself. That is why the natural bardo of this life is of the utmost importance. It is here and now that the whole preparation for all the bardos takes place. "The supreme way of preparing," it is said, "is now—to become enlightened in this lifetime."

Sometimes when I meditate, I don't use any particular method. I just allow my mind to rest, and I find, especially when I am inspired, that I can bring my mind home and relax very quickly. I sit quietly and rest in the nature of mind; I don't question or doubt whether I am in the "correct" state. There is no effort, only a rich understanding, wakefulness, and unshakable certainty.

When I am in the nature of mind, the ordinary mind is no longer there. There is no need to sustain or confirm a sense of being: *I simply am.* A fundamental trust is present. There is nothing in particular to do.

When the View is constant,
The flow of Rigpa unfailing,
And the merging of the two luminosities continuous
and spontaneous,
All possible delusion is liberated at its very root,
And your entire perception arises, without a break,
as Rigpa.

A term such as *meditation* is not really appropriate for Dzogchen practice, you can see, as ultimately it implies meditating "on" something, whereas in Dzogchen all is only and forever Rigpa. So there is no question of a meditation separate from simply abiding by the pure presence of Rigpa. The only word that could possibly describe this is *non-meditation.* In this state, the masters say, even if you look for delusion there is none left. Even if you looked for ordinary pebbles on an island of gold and jewels, you wouldn't have a chance of finding any.

August 28

If this elephant of mind is bound on all sides by the cord
    of mindfulness,
All fear disappears and complete happiness comes.
All enemies: all the tigers, lions, elephants, bears,
    serpents (of our emotions);
And all the keepers of hell; the demons and the horrors,
All of these are bound by the mastery of your mind,
And by the taming of that one mind, all are subdued,
Because from the mind are derived all fears and
    immeasurable sorrows.

SHANTIDEVA

August 29

====

Grant your blessings so that my mind may be one with the Dharma.
Grant your blessings so that Dharma may progress along the path.
Grant your blessings so that the path may clarify confusion.
Grant your blessings so that confusion may dawn as wisdom.

GAMPOPA

August 30

Each time the losses and deceptions of life teach us about impermanence, they bring us closer to the truth. When you fall from a great height, there is only one possible place to land: on the ground—the ground of truth. And if you have the understanding that comes from spiritual practice, then falling is in no way a disaster, but the discovery of an inner refuge.

August 31

Switch on the television or glance at the newspaper: You will see death everywhere. Yet, did the victims of those plane crashes and car accidents expect to die? They took life for granted, as we do. How often do we hear stories of people whom we know, or even friends, who died unexpectedly? We don't even have to be ill to die: Our bodies can suddenly break down and go out of order, just like our cars. We can be quite well one day, then fall sick and die the next.

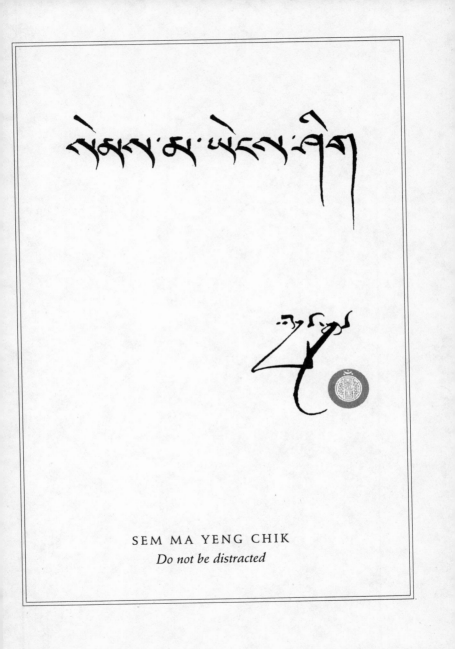

SEM MA YENG CHIK
Do not be distracted

September 1

When people begin to meditate, they often say that their thoughts are running riot and have become wilder than ever before. But I reassure them and say that this is a good sign. Far from meaning that your thoughts have become wilder, it shows that *you* have become quieter and are finally aware of just how noisy your thoughts have always been. Don't be disheartened or give up. Whatever arises, just keep being present, keep returning to the breath, even in the midst of all the confusion.

September 2

In a cloudless night sky, the full moon,
"The Lord of Stars," is about to rise. . .
The face of my compassionate lord, Padmasambhava,
Draws me on, radiating its tender welcome.

My delight in death is far, far greater than
The delight of traders at making vast fortunes at sea,
Or the lords of the gods who vaunt their victory in
  battle;
Or of those sages who have entered the rapture of
  perfect absorption.
So just as a traveler who sets out on the road when the
  time has come to go,
I will not remain in this world any longer,
But will go to dwell in the stronghold of the great bliss of
  deathlessness.

THE LAST TESTAMENT OF LONGCHENPA

September 3

There is only one way of attaining liberation and of obtaining the omniscience of enlightenment: following an authentic spiritual master. He is the guide that will help you to cross the ocean of samsara.

The sun and the moon are reflected in clear, still water instantly. Similarly, the blessings of all the buddhas are always present for those who have complete confidence in them. The sun's rays fall everywhere uniformly, but only where they are focused through a magnifying glass can they set dry grass on fire. When the all-pervading rays of the Buddha's compassion are focused through the magnifying glass of your faith and devotion, the flame of blessings blazes up in your being.

DILGO KHYENTSE RINPOCHE

Dudjom Rinpoche used to tell the story of a powerful bandit in India, who, after countless successful raids, realized the terrible suffering he had been causing. He yearned for some way of atoning for what he had done, and visited a famous master. He asked him: "I am a sinner, I am in torment. What's the way out? What can I do?"

The master looked the bandit up and down and then asked him what he was good at.

"Nothing," replied the bandit.

"Nothing?" barked the master. "You must be good at something!"

The bandit was silent for a while, and eventually admitted: "Actually there is one thing I have a talent for, and that's stealing."

The master chuckled: "Good! That's exactly the skill you'll need now. Go to a quiet place and rob all your perceptions, and steal all the stars and planets in the sky, and dissolve them into the belly of emptiness, the all-encompassing space of the nature of mind."

Within twenty-one days, the bandit had realized the nature of his mind, and eventually came to be regarded as one of the great saints of India.

September 5

When someone is suffering and you find yourself at a loss to know how to help, put yourself unflinchingly in his or her place. Imagine as vividly as possible what *you* would be going through if you were suffering the same pain. Ask yourself: "How would I feel? How would I want my friends to treat me? What would I most want from them?"

When you exchange yourself for others in this way, you are directly transferring your cherishing from its usual object, yourself, to other beings. So *exchanging yourself for others* is a very powerful way of loosening the hold on you of the self-cherishing and the self-grasping of ego, and so of releasing the heart of your compassion.

September 6

Whatever meditation method you use, drop it, or simply let it dissolve on its own, when you find that you have arrived naturally at a state of alert, expansive, and vibrant peace. Then remain there quietly, undistracted, without necessarily using any particular method. The method has already achieved its purpose. However, if you do stray or become distracted, then return to whatever technique is most appropriate to call you back.

September 7

We often wonder: "How will I be when I die?" The answer to that is that whatever state of mind we are in *now*, whatever kind of person we are now, that's what we will be like at the moment of death, if we do not change. This is why it is so absolutely important to use *this* lifetime to purify our mindstream, and so our basic being and character, while we can.

September 8

Enlightenment is real; and each of us, whoever we are, can in the right circumstances and with the right training realize the nature of mind and so know in us what is deathless and eternally pure. This is the promise of all the great mystical traditions of the world, and it has been fulfilled and is being fulfilled in countless thousands of human lives.

The wonder of this promise is that it is something not exotic, not fantastic, not for an elite, but for *all of humanity;* and when we realize it, the masters tell us, it is unexpectedly ordinary.

Spiritual truth is not something elaborate and esoteric, it is in fact profound common sense. When you realize the nature of mind, layers of confusion peel away. You don't actually "become" a buddha, you simply cease, slowly, to be deluded. And being a buddha is not being some omnipotent spiritual superman, but becoming at last a *true* human being.

Using the mantra, offer your heart and soul in fervent and one-pointed devotion, and merge and mix and blend your mind with that of Padmasambhava or your master.

Gradually you will feel yourself coming closer to Padmasambhava, and closing the gap between you and his wisdom mind. Slowly, through the blessing and power of this practice, you will find you actually experience your mind being transformed into the wisdom mind of Padmasambhava and the master: You begin to recognize their indivisibility. Just as if you put your finger into water it will get wet, and if you put it into fire it will burn, so if you invest your mind in the wisdom mind of the buddhas it will transform into their wisdom nature.

What happens is that gradually your mind begins to find itself in the state of Rigpa, as the innermost nature of mind is nothing other than the wisdom mind of all the buddhas. It is as if your ordinary mind gradually dies and dissolves, and your pure awareness, your buddha nature, your inner teacher, is revealed. This is the true meaning of "blessing"—a transformation in which your mind transcends into the state of the absolute.

Why exactly are we so frightened of death that we avoid looking at it altogether? Somewhere, deep down, we know we cannot avoid facing death forever. We know, in Milarepa's words: "This thing called 'corpse' we dread so much is living with us here and now."

September 11

The purpose of meditation is to awaken in us the skylike nature of mind, and to introduce us to that which we really are, our unchanging pure awareness that underlies the whole of life and death.

In the stillness and silence of meditation, we glimpse and return to that deep inner nature that we so long ago lost sight of amid the busyness and distraction of our minds.

Often it is only when people suddenly feel they are losing their partner that they realize how much they love them. Then they cling on even tighter. But the more they grasp, the more the other person escapes them, and the more fragile the relationship becomes.

So often we want happiness, but the very way we pursue it is so clumsy and unskillful that it brings only more sorrow. Usually we assume we must grasp in order to have that something that will ensure our happiness. We ask ourselves: "How can we possibly enjoy anything if we cannot own it?" How often attachment is mistaken for love!

Even when the relationship is a good one, love can be spoiled by attachment with its insecurity, possessiveness, and pride; and then when love is gone, all you have left to show for it are the "souvenirs" of love, the scars of attachment.

September 13

In Tibet we say: "Negative action has one good quality: it can be purified.' So there is always hope. Even murderers and the most hardened criminals can change and overcome the conditioning that led them to their crimes. Our present condition, if we use it skillfully and with wisdom, can be an inspiration to free ourselves from the bondage of suffering.

September 14

When you have explored the great mystical traditions, choose one master and follow him or her. It's one thing to set out on the spiritual journey; it's quite another to find the patience and endurance, the wisdom, courage, and humility to follow it to the end. You may have the karma to find a teacher, but you must then create the karma to follow your teacher. For very few of us know how truly to follow a master, which is an art in itself. So however great the teaching or master may be, what is essential is that you find in yourself the insight and skill to learn how to love and follow the master and the teaching.

September 15

What the world needs more than anything is bodhisattvas, active servants of peace, "clothed," as Longchenpa said, "in the armor of perseverance," dedicated to their bodhisattva vision and to the spreading of wisdom into all reaches of our experience. We need bodhisattva lawyers, bodhisattva artists and politicians, bodhisattva doctors and economists, bodhisattva teachers and scientists, bodhisattva technicians and engineers, bodhisattvas everywhere, working consciously as channels of compassion and wisdom at every level and in every situation of society; working to transform their minds and actions and those of others, working tirelessly in the certain knowledge of the support of the buddhas and enlightened beings for the preservation of our world and for a more merciful future.

September 16

If your mind is able to settle naturally of its own accord, and if you find you are inspired simply to rest in its pure awareness, then you do not need any method of meditation. However, the vast majority of us find it difficult to arrive at that state straight away. We simply do not know how to awaken it, and our minds are so wild and so distracted that we need a *skillful* means or method to evoke it.

By "skillful" I mean that you bring together your understanding of the essential nature of your mind, your knowledge of your various, shifting moods, and the insight you have developed through your practice into how to work with yourself, from moment to moment. By bringing these together, you learn the art of applying whatever method is *appropriate* to any particular situation or problem, to transform that environment of your mind.

The King Milinda once asked the Buddhist sage Nagasena: "When someone is reborn, is he the same as the one who just died, or is he different?"

Nagasena replied: "He is neither the same nor different. . . . Tell me, if a man were to light a lamp, could it provide light the whole night long?"

"Yes."

"Is the flame then which burns in the first watch of the night the same as the one that burns in the second . . . or the last?"

"No."

"Does that mean there is one lamp in the first watch of the night, another in the second, and another in the third?"

"No, it's because of that one lamp that the light shines all night."

"Rebirth is much the same: One phenomenon arises and another stops, simultaneously. So the first act of consciousness in the new existence is neither the same as the last act of consciousness in the previous existence, nor is it different."

September 18

It is important to remember always that the principle of egolessness does not mean that there was an ego in the first place but the Buddhists did away with it. On the contrary, it means *there was never any ego at all to begin with.* To realize this is called "egolessness."

September 19

Buddha was a human being, like you or me. He never claimed divinity, he merely knew he had the buddha nature, the seed of enlightenment, and that everyone else did too. The buddha nature is simply the birthright of every sentient being, and I always say: "Our buddha nature is as good as any buddha's buddha nature."

One of the greatest masters of Tonglen in Tibet was
Geshe Chekhawa, who lived in the eleventh century.
He was extremely learned and accomplished in many
forms of meditation. One day when he happened to be
in his teacher's room, he came across a book lying
open at the following lines:

> *Give all profit and gain to others,*
> *Take all loss and defeat on yourself.*

The vast and almost unimaginable compassion of
these lines astounded him and he set out to find the
master who had written them. One day on his journey
he met a leper who told him that this master had died.
But Geshe Chekhawa persevered and his long efforts
were rewarded when he found the dead master's principal disciple. Geshe Chekhawa asked this disciple:
"Just how important do you think the teachings contained in these two lines are?" The disciple replied:
"Whether you like it or not, you will have to practice
this teaching if you truly wish to attain buddhahood."

The holy secret of the practice of Tonglen is one that the mystic masters and saints of every tradition know; and living it and embodying it, with the abandon and fervor of true wisdom and true compassion, is what fills their lives with joy. One modern figure who has dedicated her life to serving the sick and dying and who radiates this joy of giving and receiving is Mother Teresa. I know of no more inspiring statement of the spiritual essence of Tonglen than these words of hers:

We all long for heaven where God is, but we have it in our power to be in heaven with Him at this very moment. But being happy with Him now means:

Loving as He loves,
Helping as He helps,
Giving as He gives,
Serving as He serves,
Rescuing as He rescues,
Being with Him twenty-four hours,
Touching Him in his distressing disguise.

September 22

Everything can be used as an invitation to meditation. A smile, a face in the subway, the sight of a small flower growing in the crack of cement pavement, a fall of rich cloth in a shop window, the way the sun lights up flower pots on a windowsill. Be alert for any sign of beauty or grace. Offer up every joy, be awake at all moments, to "the news that is always arriving out of silence."

Slowly, you will become a master of your own bliss, a chemist of your own joy, with all sorts of remedies always at hand to elevate, cheer, illuminate, and inspire your every breath and movement.

September 23

All beings have lived and died and been reborn countless times. Over and over again they have experienced the indescribable Clear Light. But because they are obscured by the darkness of ignorance, they wander endlessly in a limitless samsara.

PADMASAMBHAVA

September 24

Six realms of existence are identified in Buddhism: gods, demigods, humans, animals, hungry ghosts, and hells. They are each the result of one of the six main negative emotions: pride, jealousy, desire, ignorance, greed, and anger.

Looking at the world around us, and into our own minds, we can see that the six realms definitely do exist. They exist in the way we unconsciously allow our negative emotions to project and crystallize entire realms around us, and to define the style, form, flavor, and context of our life in those realms. And they exist also inwardly as the different seeds and tendencies of the various negative emotions within our psychophysical system, always ready to germinate and grow, depending on what influences them and how we choose to live.

September 25

When we have really grasped the law of karma in all its stark power and complex reverberations over many, many lifetimes, and seen just how our self-grasping and self-cherishing, life after life, have woven us repeatedly into a net of ignorance that seems only to be ensnaring us more and more tightly; when we have really understood the dangerous and doomed nature of the self-grasping mind's enterprise; when we have really pursued its operations into their most subtle hiding places; when we have really understood just how our whole ordinary mind and actions are defined, narrowed and darkened by it, how almost impossible it makes it for us to uncover the heart of unconditional love, and how it has blocked in us all sources of real love and real compassion, then there comes a moment when we understand, with extreme and poignant clarity, what Shantideva said:

> *If all the harms*
> *Fears and sufferings in the world*
> *Arise from self-grasping,*
> *What need have I for such a great evil spirit?*

And then a resolution is born in us to destroy that evil spirit, our greatest enemy. With that evil spirit dead, the cause of all our suffering will be removed, and our true nature, in all its spaciousness and dynamic generosity, will shine out.

September 26

To recognize the nature of your mind is to engender in the ground of your being an understanding that will change your entire worldview and help you discover and develop, naturally and spontaneously, a compassionate desire to serve all beings, as well as a direct knowledge of how best you can do so, with whatever skill or ability you have, in whatever circumstances you find yourself.

September 27

The masters stress that to stabilize the View in meditation, it is essential, first of all, to accomplish this practice in a *special environment* of retreat, where all the favorable conditions are present; amid the distractions and busyness of the world, however much you meditate, true experience will not be born in your mind.

Second, though there is no difference in Dzogchen between meditation and everyday life, until you have found true stability through doing the practice in *proper* sessions, you will not be able to integrate the wisdom of meditation into your experience of daily life.

Third, even when you practice, you might be able to abide by the continual flow of Rigpa with the confidence of the View, but if you are unable to continue that flow *at all times and in all situations,* mixing your practice with everyday life, it will not serve as a remedy when unfavorable circumstances arise, and you will be led astray into delusion by thoughts and emotions.

September 28

According to Dzogchen, the entire range of all possible appearances, and all possible phenomena in all the different realities, whether samsara or nirvana, all of these without exception have always been and will always be perfect and complete, within the vast and boundless expanse of the nature of mind. Yet, even though the essence of everything is empty and "pure from the very beginning," its nature is rich in noble qualities, pregnant with every possibility, a limitless, incessantly and dynamically creative field that is always spontaneously perfect.

September 29

When you are strong and healthy,
You never think of sickness coming,
But it descends with sudden force
Like a stroke of lightning.

When involved in worldly things,
You never think of death's approach;
Quick it comes like thunder
Crashing round your head.

MILAREPA

There is a spark of hope, a playful humor about the posture we take in meditation, which lies in the secret understanding that we all have the buddha nature. So when you assume this posture, you are playfully imitating a buddha, acknowledging and giving real encouragement to the emergence of your own buddha nature. You begin to respect yourself as a potential buddha.

At the same time, you still recognize your relative condition. But because you have let yourself be inspired by a joyful trust in your own true buddha nature, *you can accept your negative aspects more easily* and deal with them more generously and with more humor.

When you meditate, invite yourself to feel the self-esteem, the dignity, and the strong humility of the buddha that you are. If you simply let yourself be inspired by this joyful trust, it is enough: Out of this understanding and confidence, meditation will naturally arise.

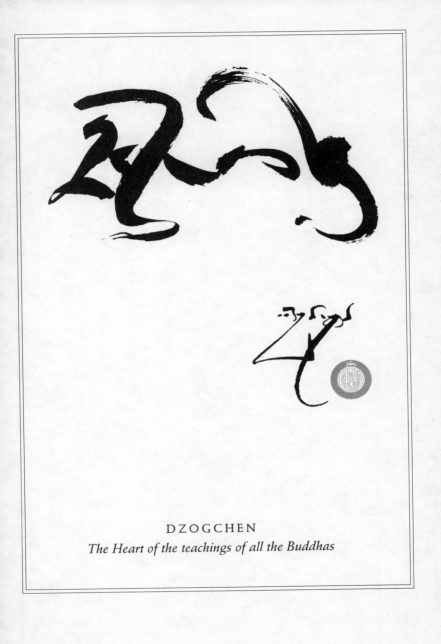

DZOGCHEN

The Heart of the teachings of all the Buddhas

October 1

You can have no greater ally in the war against your greatest enemy, your own self-grasping and self-cherishing, than the practice of compassion. It is compassion, dedicating ourselves to others, taking on their suffering instead of cherishing ourselves, that, hand in hand with the wisdom of egolessness, destroys most effectively and most completely that ancient attachment to a false self that has been the cause of our endless wandering in samsara. That is why in our tradition we see compassion as the source and essence of enlightenment and the heart of enlightened activity.

October 2

In the ancient meditation instructions, it is said that at the beginning, thoughts will arrive one on top of another, uninterrupted, like a steep mountain waterfall. Gradually, as you perfect meditation, thoughts become like the water in a deep, narrow gorge, then a great river slowly winding its way down to the sea, and finally the mind becomes like a still and placid ocean, ruffled by only the occasional ripple or wave.

October 3

We need to shake ourselves sometimes and really ask: "What if I were to die tonight? What then?" We do not know whether we will wake up tomorrow, or where. If you breathe out and you cannot breathe in again, you are dead. It's as simple as that.

As a Tibetan saying goes: "Tomorrow or the next life—which comes first, we never know."

October 4

It is said that when Buddha attained enlightenment, all he wanted to do was to show the rest of us the nature of mind and share completely what he had realized. But he also saw, with the great sorrow of infinite compassion, how difficult it would be for us to understand.

For even though we have the same inner nature as Buddha, we have not recognized it because it is so enclosed and wrapped up in our individual ordinary minds.

Imagine an empty vase. The space inside is exactly the same as the space outside. Only the fragile walls of the vase separate one from the other. Our buddha mind is enclosed within the walls of our ordinary mind. But when we become enlightened, it is as if the vase shatters into pieces. The space "inside" merges instantly into the space "outside." They become one: There and then we realize that they were never separate or different; *they were always the same.*

October 5

All the spiritual teachers of humanity have told us the same thing, that the purpose of life on earth is to achieve union with our fundamental, enlightened nature. It says in the Upanishads:

There is the path of wisdom and the path of ignorance. They are far apart and lead to different ends. . . . Abiding in the midst of ignorance, thinking themselves wise and learned, fools go aimlessly hither and thither like the blind led by the blind. What lies beyond life shines not to those who are childish, or careless, or deluded by wealth.

October 6

One technique for arousing compassion for a person who is suffering is to imagine one of your dearest friends, or someone you really love, in that person's place.

Imagine your brother or daughter or parent or best friend in the same kind of painful situation. Quite naturally your heart will open, and compassion will awaken in you: What more would you want than to free your loved one from his or her torment? Now take this compassion released in your heart and transfer it to the person who needs your help: You will find that your help is inspired more naturally and that you can direct it more easily.

October 7

The real glory of meditation lies not in any method but in its continual living experience of presence, in its bliss, clarity, peace, and, most important of all, complete absence of grasping.

The diminishing of your grasping is a sign that you are becoming freer of yourself. And the more you experience this freedom, the clearer the sign that the ego and the hopes and fears that keep it alive are dissolving and the closer you will come to the infinitely generous "wisdom of egolessness." When you live in that wisdom home, you'll no longer find a barrier between "I" and "you," "this" and "that," "inside" and "outside"; you'll have come, finally, to your true home, the state of nonduality.

October 8

I remember a middle-aged American woman who came to see Dudjom Rinpoche in New York in 1976. She came into the room, and sat in front of Dudjom Rinpoche, and blurted out: "My doctor has given me only a few months to live. Can you help me? I am dying."

To her surprise, in a gentle yet compassionate way, Dudjom Rinpoche began to chuckle. Then he said quietly: "You see, we are all dying. It's only a matter of time. Some of us just die sooner than others."

With these few words, he helped her to see the universality of death, and that her impending death was not unique. This eased her anxiety. Then he talked to her about dying and the acceptance of death. And he spoke about the hope there is in death. At the end, he gave her a healing practice that she followed enthusiastically. Not only did she come to accept death, but, by following the practice with complete dedication, she recovered her health.

October 9

One of the greatest Buddhist traditions calls the nature of mind "the wisdom of ordinariness." I cannot say it enough: Our true nature and the nature of all beings is not something extraordinary.

The irony is that it is our so-called ordinary world that is extraordinary, a fantastic, elaborate hallucination of the deluded vision of samsara. It is this "extraordinary" vision that blinds us to the "ordinary," natural, inherent nature of mind. Imagine if the buddhas were looking down at us now: How they would marvel sadly at the lethal ingenuity and intricacy of our confusion!

October 10

Once there was a Dzogchen yogi who lived unostentatiously, surrounded, however, by a large following of disciples. A certain monk, who had an exaggerated opinion of his own learning and scholarship, was jealous of the yogi, whom he knew not to be very well read at all. He thought: "How does he, just an ordinary person, dare to teach? How dare he pretend to be a master? I will go and test his knowledge, show it up for the sham it is, and humiliate him in front of his disciples, so that they will leave him and follow me."

One day he visited the yogi and said scornfully: "You Dzogchen bunch, is meditate *all* you ever do?"

The yogi's reply took him completely by surprise: "What is there to meditate on?"

"You don't even meditate then," the scholar brayed triumphantly.

"But when am I *ever* distracted?" said the yogi.

Isn't it extraordinary that our minds cannot stay still for longer than a few moments without grasping after distraction? They are so restless and preoccupied that sometimes I think that living in a city in the modern world, we are already like the tormented beings in the intermediate state after death, where the consciousness is said to be agonizingly restless.

We are fragmented into so many different aspects. We don't know who we really are, or what aspects of ourselves we should identify with or believe in. So many contradictory voices, dictates, and feelings fight for control over our inner lives that we find ourselves scattered everywhere, in all directions, leaving nobody at home.

Meditation, then, is bringing the mind home.

October 12

As Buddha said: "What you are is what you have been, what you will be is what you do now." Padmasambhava went further: "If you want to know your past life, look into your present condition; if you want to know your future life, look at your present actions."

October 13

When the teachings "click" for you somewhere deep in your heart and mind, then you really have the View. Whatever difficulties you face, you will find you have some kind of serenity, stability, and understanding, and an internal mechanism—you could call it an "inner transformer"—that works for you, to protect you from falling prey to wrong views. In that View, you will have discovered a "wisdom guide" of your own, always on hand to advise you, support you, and remind you of the truth. Confusion will still arise, that's only normal, but with a crucial difference: No longer will you focus on it in a blinded and obsessive way, but you will look on it with humor, perspective, and compassion.

The fear that impermanence awakens in us, that nothing is real and nothing lasts, is, we come to discover, our greatest friend because it drives us to ask: If everything dies and changes, then what is really true? Is there something *behind* the appearances? Is there something in fact we *can* depend on, that does survive what we call death?

Allowing these questions to occupy us urgently, and reflecting on them, we slowly find ourselves making a profound shift in the way we view everything. We come to uncover in ourselves "something" that we begin to realize lies behind all the changes and deaths of the world.

As this happens, we catch repeated and glowing glimpses of the vast implications behind the truth of impermanence. We come to uncover a depth of peace, joy, and confidence in ourselves that fills us with wonder, and breeds in us gradually a certainty that there is in us "something" that nothing destroys, that nothing alters, and that cannot die.

October 15

Whatever is happening to us now mirrors our past karma. If we know that, and know it truly, whenever suffering and difficulties befall us, we do not view them particularly as failures or catastrophes, or see suffering as a punishment in any way. Nor do we blame ourselves or indulge in self-hatred.

We see the pain we are going through as the completion of the effects, the fruition, of a past karma. Tibetans say that suffering is "a broom that sweeps away all our negative karma." We can even be grateful that one karma is coming to an end. We know that "good fortune," a fruit of good karma, may soon pass if we do not use it well, and that "misfortune," the result of negative karma, may in fact be giving us a marvelous opportunity to evolve.

October 16

Some day, after we have mastered the winds, the waves, the tides and gravity, . . . we shall harness . . . the energies of love. Then, for the second time in the history of the world, man will have discovered fire.

TEILHARD DE CHARDIN

October 17

The belief in reincarnation shows us that there is some kind of ultimate justice or goodness in the universe. It is that goodness that we are all trying to uncover and to free. Whenever we act positively, we move toward it; whenever we act negatively, we obscure and inhibit it. And whenever we cannot express it in our lives and actions, we feel miserable and frustrated.

October 18

The way to discover the freedom of the wisdom of egolessness, the masters advise us, is through the process of listening and hearing, contemplation and reflection, and meditation. They advise us to begin by *listening* repeatedly to the spiritual teachings. As we listen, they will keep on and on reminding us of our hidden wisdom nature.

Gradually, as we listen to the teachings, certain passages and insights in them will strike a strange chord in us, memories of our true nature will start to trickle back to us, and a deep feeling of something homely and uncannily familiar will slowly awaken.

October 19

Remember: A method is only a means, *not* the meditation itself. It is through practicing the method skillfully that you reach the perfection of that *pure state of total presence,* which is the real meditation.

There is a revealing Tibetan saying: "Gompa ma yin, kompa yin," which means literally: "*Meditation* is not; *getting used to* is."

It means that meditation is nothing other than getting used to the *practice* of meditation. As it is said: "Meditation is not striving, but naturally becoming assimilated into it." As you continue to practice the method, then meditation slowly arises. Meditation is not something that you can "do"; it is something that has to happen spontaneously, only when you have perfected the practice.

October 20

If we were to put our minds to one powerful wisdom method and work with it directly, there is a real possibility we would become enlightened.

Our minds, however, are riddled with confusion and doubt. I sometimes think that doubt is an even greater block to human evolution than is desire or attachment. Our society promotes cleverness instead of wisdom, and celebrates the most superficial, harsh, and least useful aspects of our intelligence. We have become so falsely "sophisticated" and neurotic that we take doubt itself for truth, and the doubt that is nothing more than ego's desperate attempt to defend itself from wisdom is deified as the goal and fruit of true knowledge.

This form of mean-spirited doubt is the shabby emperor of samsara, served by a flock of "experts" who teach us not the open-souled and generous doubt that Buddha assured us was necessary for testing and proving the worth of the teachings, but a destructive form of doubt that leaves us nothing to believe in, nothing to hope for, and nothing to live by.

So many veils and illusions separate us from the stark knowledge that we are dying. When we finally know we are dying, and all other sentient beings are dying with us, we start to have a burning, almost heartbreaking sense of the fragility and preciousness of each moment and each being, and from this can grow a deep, clear, limitless compassion for all beings.

Sir Thomas More, I heard, wrote these words just before his beheading: "We are all in the same cart, going to execution; how can I hate anyone or wish anyone harm?" To feel the full force of your mortality, and to open your heart entirely to it, is to allow to grow in you that all-encompassing, fearless compassion that fuels the lives of all those who wish truly to be of help to others.

What is a great spiritual practitioner? A person who lives always in the presence of his or her own true self, someone who has found and who uses continually the springs and sources of profound inspiration. As the modern English writer Lewis Thompson wrote: "Christ, supreme poet, lived truth so passionately that every gesture of his, at once pure Act and perfect Symbol, embodies the transcendent."

To embody the transcendent is why we are here.

October 23

When little obstacles crop up on the spiritual path, a good practitioner does not lose faith and begin to doubt, but has the discernment to recognize difficulties, whatever they may be, for what they are—just obstacles, and nothing more. It is the nature of things that when you recognize an obstacle as such, it ceases to be an obstacle. Equally, it is by failing to recognize an obstacle for what it is, and therefore taking it seriously, that it is empowered and solidified and becomes a real blockage.

The quality of life in the realm of the gods may look superior to our own, yet the masters tell us that human life is infinitely more valuable. Why? Because of the very fact that we have the awareness and intelligence that are the raw materials for enlightenment, and because the very suffering that pervades this human realm is itself the spur to spiritual transformation.

Pain, grief, loss, and ceaseless frustration of every kind are there for a very real and dramatic purpose: to wake us up, to enable, almost to force us to break out of the cycle of samsara and so release our imprisoned splendor.

October 25

It has often intrigued me how some Buddhist masters I know ask one simple question of people who approach them for teaching: "Do you believe in a life after this one?" They are not being asked whether they believe in it as a philosophical proposition but whether they feel it deeply in their hearts. The master knows that if a man believes in a life after this one, his whole outlook on life will be different, and he will have a distinct sense of personal responsibility and morality. What the masters must suspect is that there is a danger that people who have no strong belief in a life after this one will create a society fixated on short-term results, without much thought for the consequences of their actions.

Could this be the major reason why we have created a world like the one we are now living in, a world with hardly any real compassion?

October 26

Feeling the living presence of Buddha, of Padmasam-bhava, of your master, and simply opening your heart and mind to the embodiment of truth, really does bless and transform your mind. As you invoke Buddha, your own buddha nature is inspired to awaken and blossom, as naturally as a flower in sunlight.

October 27

Dilgo Khyentse Rinpoche describes a yogi wandering through a garden. He is completely awake to the splendor and beauty of the flowers, and relishes their colors, shapes and scents. But there is no trace of clinging or any "after-thought" in his mind.

As Dudjom Rinpoche says:

"Whatever perceptions arise, you should be like a little child going into a beautifully decorated temple; he looks, but grasping does not enter into his perception at all. You leave everything fresh, natural, vivid and unspoiled. When you leave each thing in its own state, then its shape doesn't change, its color doesn't fade and its glow does not disappear. Whatever appears is unstained by any grasping, so then all that you perceive arises as the naked wisdom of Rigpa, which is the indivisibility of luminosity and emptiness."

Things will never be perfect. How could they be? We are still in samsara. Even when you have chosen your master and are following the teachings as sincerely as you can, you will meet difficulties and frustrations, contradictions and imperfections. Don't succumb to obstacles and tiny difficulties. These are often only ego's childish emotions. Don't let them blind you to the essential and enduring value of what you have chosen. Don't let your impatience drag you away from your commitment to the truth.

I have been saddened, again and again, to see how many people take up a teaching or a master with enthusiasm and promise, only to lose heart when the smallest, unavoidable obstacles arise, then tumble back into samsara and old habits, and waste years or perhaps a lifetime.

October 29

Compassion is not true compassion unless it is active. Avalokiteshvara, the Buddha of Compassion, is often represented in Tibetan iconography as having a thousand eyes that see the pain in all corners of the universe, and a thousand arms to reach out to all corners of the universe to extend his help.

October 30

When you meditate, breathe naturally, just as you always do.

Focus your awareness lightly on the outbreath. When you breathe out, just flow out with the out-breath. Each time you breathe out, you are letting go and releasing all your grasping. Imagine your breath dissolving into the all-pervading expanse of truth.

Each time you breathe out, and before you breathe in again, you will find that there is a natural gap, as your grasping dissolves.

Rest in that gap, in that open space. And when, naturally, you breathe in, don't focus especially on the in-breath but go on resting your mind in the gap that has opened up.

October 31

The teachings show us precisely what will happen if we prepare for death and what will happen if we do not. The choice could not be clearer. If we refuse to accept death now, while we are still alive, we will pay dearly throughout our lives, at the moment of death, and thereafter. The effects of this refusal will ravage this life and all the lives to come.

We will not be able to live our lives fully; we will remain imprisoned in the very aspect of ourselves that has to die. This ignorance will rob us of the basis of the journey to enlightenment, and trap us endlessly in the realm of illusion, the uncontrolled cycle of birth and death, that ocean of suffering that Buddhists call "samsara."

HŪṂ
The Wisdom Mind of all the Buddhas

November 1

Taking life seriously does not mean spending our whole lives meditating as if we were living in the Himalaya Mountains or in the old days in Tibet. In the modern world, we have to work to earn our living, but we should not get entangled in a nine-to-five existence, where we live without any view of the deeper meaning of life.

Our task is to strike a balance, to find a middle way, to learn not to overextend ourselves with extraneous activities and preoccupations, but to simplify our lives more and more. *The key to finding a happy balance in modern life is simplicity.*

November 2

What need is there to say more?
The childish work for their own benefit,
The buddhas work for the benefit of others.
Just look at the difference between them.

If I do not exchange my happiness
For the suffering of others,
I shall not attain the state of buddhahood
And even in samsara I shall have no real joy.

SHANTIDEVA

November 3

When you are practicing meditation, it's important not to get involved in mental commentary, analysis, or internal gossip. Do not mistake the running commentary in your mind ("Now I'm breathing in, now I'm breathing out") for mindfulness; what is important is pure presence.

Don't concentrate too much on the breath; give it about 25 percent of your attention, with the other 75 percent quietly and spaciously relaxed. As you become more mindful of your breathing, you will find that you become more and more present, gather all your scattered aspects back into yourself, and become whole.

November 4

The fundamental message of the Buddhist teachings is that if we are prepared, there is tremendous hope, both in life and in death. The teachings reveal to us the possibility of an astounding and finally boundless freedom, which is ours to work for now, in life—the freedom that will also enable us to choose our death and so to choose our next birth.

For someone who has prepared and practiced, death comes not as a defeat but as a triumph, the crowning and most glorious moment of life.

November 5

GENERATION OF BODDHICITTA

Ho! Mesmerised by the sheer variety of perceptions,
*   which*
are like the illusory reflections of the moon in water,
Beings wander endlessly astray in samsara's vicious
*   cycle.*
In order that they may find comfort and ease in the
*   luminosity*
and all-pervading space of the true nature of their
*   minds,*
I generate the immeasurable love, compassion, joy and
*   equanimity*
of the awakened mind, the heart of Bodhicitta.

JIKMÉ LINGPA

November 6

Our buddha nature has an active aspect, which is our "inner teacher." From the very moment we became obscured, this "inner teacher" has worked tirelessly for us, tirelessly trying to bring us back to the radiance and spaciousness of our true being. Not for one second, my master Jamyang Khyentse said, has the inner teacher given up on us. In its infinite compassion, one with the infinite compassion of all the buddhas and all the enlightened beings, it has been ceaselessly working for our evolution—not only in this life but in all our past lives—using all kinds of skillful means and all types of situations to teach and awaken us and to guide us back to the truth.

November 7

Is karma really so hard to see in operation? Don't we only have to look back at our own lives to see clearly the consequences of some of our actions? When we upset or hurt someone, didn't it rebound on us? Were we not left with a bitter and dark memory, and the shadows of self-disgust? That memory and those shadows are karma. Our habits and our fears too are also due to karma, the results of our past actions, words, and thoughts. If we examine our actions, and become really mindful of them, we will see that there is a pattern that repeats itself. *Whenever we act negatively, it leads to pain and suffering; whenever we act positively, it eventually results in happiness.*

November 8

For us to survive on the spiritual path, there are many challenges to face, and there is much to learn. We have to discover how to deal with obstacles and difficulties; how to process doubts and see through wrong views; how to inspire ourselves when we least feel like it; how to understand ourselves and our moods; how really to work with and integrate the teachings and practices; how to evoke compassion and enact it in life; and how to transform our suffering and emotions.

On the spiritual path, all of us need the support and the good foundation that come from really knowing the teachings, and this cannot be stressed strongly enough. For the more we study and practice, the more we shall embody discernment, clarity, and insight. Then, when the truth comes knocking, we will know it, with certainty, for what it is, and gladly open the door, because we'll have guessed that it may well be the truth of who we really are.

November 9

Meditation is bringing the mind back home, and this is first achieved through the practice of mindfulness.

Once an old woman came to Buddha and asked him how to meditate. He told her to remain aware of every movement of her hands as she drew water from the well, knowing that if she did, she would soon find herself in that state of alert and spacious calm that is meditation.

November 10

Evoking the power of compassion in us is not always easy. I find myself that the simplest ways are the best and the most direct. Every day, life gives us innumerable chances to open our hearts, if we can only take them. An old woman passes you with a sad and lonely face and two heavy plastic bags full of shopping she can hardly carry. Switch on a television, and there on the news is a mother in Beirut kneeling above the body of her murdered son, or an old grandmother in Moscow pointing to the thin soup that is her *only* food. . . .

Any one of these sights could open the eyes of your heart to the fact of vast suffering in the world. Let it. Don't waste the love and grief it arouses. In the moment you feel compassion welling up in you, don't brush it aside, don't shrug it off and try quickly to return to "normal," don't be afraid of your feeling or be embarrassed by it, and don't allow yourself to be distracted from it. Be vulnerable: Use that quick, bright uprush of compassion—focus on it, go deep into your heart and meditate on it, develop it, enhance and deepen it. By doing this you will realize how blind you have been to suffering.

All beings, everywhere, suffer; let your heart go out to them all in spontaneous and immeasurable compassion.

November 11

Often people ask me: "How long should I meditate? And when? Should I practice twenty minutes in the morning and in the evening, or is it better to do several short practices during the day?" Yes, it is good to meditate for twenty minutes, though that is not to say that twenty minutes is the limit. I have not found in the scriptures any reference to twenty minutes; I think it is a notion that has been contrived in the West, and I call it Meditation Western Standard Time.

The point is not how long you meditate; the point is whether the practice actually brings you to a certain state of mindfulness and presence, where you are a little open and able to connect with your heart essence. And five minutes of wakeful sitting practice is of far greater value than twenty minutes of dozing!

November 12

As Buddha said in his first teaching, the root of all our suffering in samsara is *ignorance*. Ignorance, until we free ourselves from it, can seem endless, and even when we have embarked on the spiritual path our search is fogged by it. However, if you remember this, and keep the teachings in your heart, you will gradually develop the discernment to recognize the innumerable confusions of ignorance for what they are, and so never jeopardize your commitment or lose your perspective.

Every spiritual tradition has stressed that this human life is unique and has a potential that ordinarily we don't even begin to imagine. If we miss the opportunity this life offers us for transforming ourselves, they say, it may well be an extremely long time before we have another.

Imagine a blind turtle roaming the depths of an ocean the size of the universe. Up above floats a wooden ring, tossed to and fro on the waves. Every hundred years, the turtle comes, once, to the surface. To be born a human being is said by Buddhists to be *more* difficult than for that turtle to surface accidentally with its head poking through the wooden ring.

And even among those who have a human birth, it is said, those who have the great good fortune to make a connection with the teachings are rare, and those who really take them to heart and embody them in their actions even rarer—as rare, in fact, "as stars in broad daylight."

November 14

Because in our culture we overvalue the intellect, we imagine that to become enlightened demands extraordinary intelligence. In fact, many kinds of cleverness are just further obscurations. There is a Tibetan saying: "If you are too clever, you could miss the point entirely."

Patrul Rinpoche said: "The logical mind seems interesting, but it is the seed of delusion." People can become obsessed with their own theories and miss the point of everything. In Tibet we say: "Theories are like patches on a coat, one day they just wear off."

November 15

Although we have been made to believe that if we let go we will end up with nothing, life itself reveals again and again the opposite: that letting go is the path to real freedom.

Just as when the waves lash at the shore, the rocks suffer no damage but are sculpted and eroded into beautiful shapes, so our characters can be molded and our rough edges worn smooth by changes. Through weathering changes, we can learn how to develop a gentle but unshakable composure. Our confidence in ourselves grows, and becomes so much greater that goodness and compassion begin naturally to radiate out from us and bring joy to others.

That goodness is what survives death, a fundamental goodness that is in each and every one of us. The whole of our life is a teaching of how to uncover that strong goodness, and a training toward realizing it.

Let's not take doubts with exaggerated seriousness, or let them grow out of proportion, so that we become black-and-white or fanatical about them. What we need to learn is how slowly to change our culturally conditioned and passionate involvement with doubt into a free, humorous, and compassionate one. This means giving doubts time, and giving ourselves time to find answers to our questions that are not merely intellectual or "philosophical" but living and real and genuine and workable.

Doubts cannot resolve themselves immediately; but if we are patient, a space can be created within us in which doubts can be carefully and objectively examined, unraveled, dissolved, and healed. What we lack, especially in this culture, is the right, undistracted, and richly spacious environment of the mind, which can be created only through sustained meditation practice, and in which insights can be given the chance slowly to mature and ripen.

November 17

The birth of a man is the birth of his sorrow. The longer he lives, the more stupid he becomes, because his anxiety to avoid unavoidable death becomes more and more acute. What bitterness! He lives for what is always out of reach! His thirst for survival in the future makes him incapable of living in the present.

CHUANG TZU

November 18

Those who have been through the near-death experience have reported a startling range of aftereffects and changes. One woman said:

The things that I felt slowly were a very heightened sense of love, the ability to communicate love, the ability to find joy and pleasures in the smallest and most insignificant things about me. . . . I developed a great compassion for people that were ill and facing death and I wanted so much to let them know, to somehow make them aware that the dying process was nothing more than an extension of one's life.

November 19

When we have prayed and aspired and hungered for the truth for a long time, for many, many lives, and when our karma has become sufficiently purified, a kind of miracle takes place. And this miracle, if we can understand and use it, can lead to the ending of ignorance forever: The inner teacher, who has been with us always, manifests in the form of the "outer teacher," who, almost as if by magic, we actually encounter. This is the most important encounter of any lifetime.

November 20

Body lying flat on a last bed,
Voices whispering a few last words,
Mind watching a final memory glide past:
When will that drama come for you?

VIITH DALAI LAMA

November 21

Karma means that whatever we do, with our bodies, speech, or minds, will have a corresponding result. Each action, even the smallest, is pregnant with its consequences. It is said by the masters that even a little poison can cause death, and even a tiny seed can become a huge tree. And as Buddha said: "Do not overlook negative actions merely because they are small; however small a spark may be, it can burn down a haystack as big as a mountain."

Similarly he said: "Do not overlook tiny good actions, thinking they are of no benefit; even tiny drops of water in the end will fill a huge vessel."

Karma does not decay like external things, or ever become inoperative. It cannot be destroyed "by time, fire, or water." Its power will never disappear, until it is ripened.

November 22

O love, O pure deep love, be here, be now
Be all; worlds dissolve into your stainless endless
   radiance,
Frail living leaves burn with you brighter than cold
   stars:
Make me your servant, your breath, your core.

RUMI

November 23

The Buddha summons us to a different kind of doubt, "like analyzing gold, scorching, cutting and rubbing it to test its purity." For this form of doubt really exposes us to the truth if we follow it to the end, but we have neither the insight, the courage, nor the training. We have been schooled in a sterile addiction to contradiction that has robbed us repeatedly of all real openness to any more expansive and ennobling truth.

In the place of our contemporary nihilistic form of doubt I would ask you to put what I call a "noble doubt," the kind that is an integral part of the path toward enlightenment. The vast truth of the mystical teachings handed down to us is not something that our endangered world can afford to dismiss. Instead of doubting *them,* why don't we doubt ourselves: our ignorance, our assumption that we understand everything already, our grasping and evasion, our passion for so-called explanations of reality that have about them nothing of the awe-inspiring and all-encompassing wisdom of what the masters, the messengers of Reality, have told us?

November 24

We may say, and even half-believe, that compassion is marvelous, but in practice our actions are deeply un-compassionate and bring us and others mostly frustration and distress, and not the happiness we are all seeking.

Isn't it absurd that we all long for happiness, yet nearly all our actions and feelings lead us directly away from that happiness?

What do we imagine will make us happy? A canny, self-seeking, resourceful selfishness, the selfish protection of ego, which can, as we all know, make us at moments extremely brutal. But in fact the complete reverse is true: Self-grasping and self-cherishing are seen, when you really look at them, to be the root of all harm to others, and also of all harm to ourselves.

November 25

Sometimes people think that when they meditate there should be no thoughts and emotions at all; and when thoughts and emotions do arise, they become annoyed and exasperated with themselves and think they have failed. Nothing could be further from the truth. There is a Tibetan saying: "It's a tall order to ask for meat without bones, and tea without leaves." As long as you have a mind, you will have thoughts and emotions.

November 26

Confined in the dark, narrow cage of our own making that we take for the whole universe, very few of us can even begin to imagine another dimension of mind. Patrul Rinpoche tells the story of an old frog who had lived all his life in a dank well. One day a frog from the sea paid him a visit.

"Where do you come from?" asked the frog in the well.

"From the great ocean," he replied.

"How big is your ocean?"

"It's gigantic."

"You mean about a quarter of the size of my well here?"

"Bigger."

"Bigger? You mean half as big?"

"No, even bigger."

"Is it . . . as big as this well?"

"There's no comparison."

"That's impossible! I've got to see this for myself."

They set off together. When the frog from the well saw the ocean, it was such a shock that his head just exploded into pieces.

November 27

Whatever our lives are like, our buddha nature is always there. And it is always perfect. We say that not even the buddhas can improve it in their infinite wisdom, nor can sentient beings spoil it in their seemingly infinite confusion.

Our true nature could be compared to the sky, and the confusion of the ordinary mind to clouds. Some days the sky is completely obscured by clouds. When we are down on the ground, looking up, it is very difficult to believe that there is anything else there but clouds. Yet we have only to fly in a plane to discover above the clouds a limitless expanse of clear blue sky. From up there, the clouds we assumed were everything seem so small and so far away down below.

We should always try to remember: The clouds are not the sky and do not "belong" to it. They only hang there and pass by in their slightly ridiculous and nondependent fashion. And they can never stain or mark the sky in any way.

November 28

Action is being truly observant of your own thoughts, good or bad, looking into the true nature of whatever thoughts may arise, neither tracing the past nor inviting the future, neither allowing any clinging to experiences of joy, nor being overcome by sad situations. In so doing, you try to reach and remain in the state of great equilibrium, where all good and bad, peace and distress, are devoid of true identity.

DUDJOM RINPOCHE

You can think of the nature of mind like a mirror, with five different powers or "wisdoms." Its openness and vastness is the "wisdom of all-encompassing space," the womb of compassion. Its capacity to reflect in precise detail whatever comes before it is the "mirrorlike wisdom." Its fundamental lack of any bias toward any impression is the "equalizing wisdom." Its ability to distinguish clearly, without confusing in any way the various different phenomena that arise, is the "wisdom of discernment." And its potential of having everything already accomplished, perfected, and spontaneously present is the "all-accomplishing wisdom."

For meditation to happen, calm and auspicious conditions have to be created. Before we have mastery over our minds, we need first to calm their environment.

At the moment, our minds are like a candle flame: unstable, flickering, constantly changing, fanned by the violent winds of our thoughts and emotions. The flame will burn steadily only when we can calm the air around it; so we can only begin to glimpse and rest in the nature of mind when we have stilled the turbulence of our thoughts and emotions. On the other hand, once we have found a stability in our meditation, noises and disturbances of every kind will have far less impact.

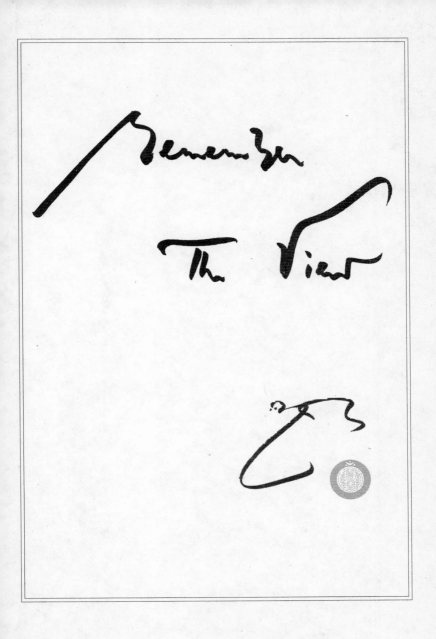

December 1

The beginner's mind is an open mind, an empty mind, a ready mind, and if we really listen with a beginner's mind, we might really begin to hear. For if we listen with a silent mind, as free as possible from the clamor of preconceived ideas, a possibility will be created for the truth of the teachings to pierce us, and for the meaning of life and death to become increasingly and startlingly clear.

My master Dilgo Khyentse Rinpoche said: "The more and more you listen, the more and more you hear; the more and more you hear, the deeper and deeper your understanding becomes."

December 2

Gradually, as you remain open and mindful, and use a technique to focus your mind more and more, your negativity will slowly be defused; you begin to feel well in your own skin, or, as the French say, *être bien dans sa peau* ("well in your own skin"). From this comes release and a profound ease. I think of this practice as the most effective form of therapy and self-healing.

December 3

Every single negative thing we have ever thought or done has ultimately arisen from our *grasping at a false self,* and our *cherishing of that false self,* making it the dearest and most important element in our lives. All those negative thoughts, emotions, desires, and actions that are the cause of our negative karma are engendered by self-grasping and self-cherishing. They are the dark, powerful magnet that attracts to us, life after life, every obstacle, every misfortune, every anguish, every disaster, and so they are the root cause of all the sufferings of samsara.

December 4

It is important to reflect calmly, again and again, that *death is real and comes without warning.*

Don't be like the pigeon in the Tibetan proverb: He spends all night fussing about, making his bed, and dawn comes up before he has even had time to go to sleep.

December 5

Realizing the View subtly but completely transforms your vision of everything. More and more, I have come to realize how thoughts and concepts are *all* that block us from always being, quite simply, in the absolute.

Now I see clearly why the masters so often say: "Try hard not to create too much hope and fear," for they only engender more mental gossip. When the View is there, thoughts are seen for what they truly are: fleeting and transparent, and only relative. You see through everything directly, as if you had X-ray eyes. You do not cling to thoughts and emotions or reject them; you welcome them all within the vast embrace of Rigpa. The things you took so seriously before—ambitions, plans, expectations, doubts, and passions—no longer have any deep and anxious hold on you, for the View has helped you to see the futility and pointlessness of them all, and born in you a spirit of true renunciation.

December 6

Devotion is the purest, quickest, and simplest way to realize the nature of mind and all things. As we progress in it, the process reveals itself as wonderfully interdependent: We, from our side, try continually to generate devotion, which itself generates glimpses of the nature of mind, and these glimpses only enhance and deepen our devotion to the master who is inspiring us. So in the end devotion springs out of wisdom: devotion and the living experience of the nature of mind become inseparable and inspire each other.

December 7

What is our life but a dance of transient forms? Isn't everything always changing? Doesn't everything we have done in the past seem like a dream now? The friends we grew up with, the childhood haunts, those views and opinions we once held with such single-minded passion: We have left them all behind. Now, at this moment, reading this book seems vividly real to you. Even this page will soon be only a memory.

December 8

When you practice meditation, rather than "watching" the breath, let yourself gradually identify with it, as if you were becoming it. Slowly the breath, the breather, and the breathing become one; duality and separation dissolve.

You will find that this very simple process of mindfulness filters your thoughts and emotions. Then, as if you were shedding an old skin, something is peeled off and freed.

December 9

Sit quietly. From the depths of your heart, invoke in the sky in front of you the embodiment of the truth in the person of your master, a saint, or an enlightened being.

Try to visualize the master or buddha as alive and as radiant and translucent as a rainbow.

If you have difficulty visualizing the master, imagine the embodiment of truth simply as light, or try to feel his or her perfect presence there in the sky before you. Let all the inspiration, joy, and awe you then feel take the place of visualization. My master Dudjom Rinpoche used to say that it does not matter if you cannot visualize; what is more important is to feel the presence in your heart, and to know that this presence embodies the blessings, compassion, energy, and wisdom of all the buddhas.

With deep devotion, merge your mind with the master's, then rest your mind in his or her wisdom mind.

December 10

Life, as Buddha told us, is as brief as a lightning flash; yet, as Wordsworth said: "The world is too much with us: Getting and spending, we lay waste our powers." It is that laying waste of our powers—that betrayal of our essence, that abandonment of the miraculous chance that this life, the natural bardo, gives us of knowing and embodying our enlightened nature—that is perhaps the most heartbreaking thing about human life. What the masters are essentially telling us is to stop fooling ourselves: What will we have learned, if at the moment of death we do not know who we really are?

December 11

We must never forget that it is through our actions, words, and thoughts that we have a choice. And if we choose to do so, we can put an end to suffering and the causes of suffering, and help our true potential, our buddha nature, to awaken in us. Until this buddha nature is completely awakened and we are freed from our ignorance and merge with the deathless, enlightened mind, there can be no end to the round of life and death. So, the teachings tell us, if we do not assume the fullest possible responsibility for ourselves now in this life, our suffering will go on not only for a few lives but for thousands of lives.

It is this sobering knowledge that makes Buddhists consider that future lives are more important even than this one, because there are many more that await us in the future. This long-term vision governs how they live. They know if we were to sacrifice the whole of eternity for this life, it would be like spending our entire life savings on one drink, madly ignoring the consequences.

December 12

It may be surprising for the West to learn how very many incarnations there have been in Tibet, and how the majority have been great masters, scholars, authors, mystics, and saints who made an outstanding contribution both to the teaching of Buddhism and to society. They played a central role in the history of Tibet.

I believe that this process of incarnation is not limited to Tibet but can occur in all countries and at all times. Throughout history there have been people of artistic genius, spiritual strength, and humanitarian vision who have helped the human race to go forward. I think of Gandhi, Einstein, Abraham Lincoln, Mother Teresa, of Shakespeare, of Saint Francis, of Beethoven and Michelangelo.

When Tibetans hear of such people, they immediately say they are bodhisattvas. And whenever I hear of them, of their work and vision, I am moved by the majesty of the vast evolutionary process of the buddhas and masters that emanate to liberate beings and better the world.

December 13

Doubt is not a disease but merely a symptom of a lack of what we in our tradition call the View, which is the realization of the nature of mind, and so of the nature of reality. When the View is there completely, there will be no possibility for the slightest trace of doubt, for then we'll be looking at reality through its own eyes. But until we reach enlightenment there will inevitably be doubts, because doubt is a fundamental activity of the unenlightened mind, and *the only way to deal with doubts is neither to suppress nor indulge them.*

December 14

To realize what I call the wisdom of compassion is to see with complete clarity its benefits, as well as the damage that its opposite has done to us. We need to make a very clear distinction between what is in our *ego's self-interest* and what is in *our ultimate interest;* it is from mistaking one for the other that all our suffering comes.

Self-grasping creates self-cherishing, which in turn creates an ingrained aversion to harm and suffering. However, harm and suffering have no objective existence; what gives them their existence and their power is only our aversion to them. When you understand this, you understand then that it is our aversion that attracts to us every negativity and obstacle that can possibly happen to us, and fills our lives with nervous anxiety, expectation, and fear.

Wear down that aversion by wearing down the self-grasping mind and its attachment to a nonexistent self, and you will wear down any hold on you that any obstacle and negativity can have. For how can you attack someone or something that is just not there?

December 15

Each time we begin our practice of meditation, we are moved by the awareness that we and all other sentient beings fundamentally have the buddha nature as our innermost essence, and that to realize it is to be free of ignorance and to put an end, finally, to suffering.

We are inspired with the motivation to dedicate our practice, and our life, to the enlightenment of all beings in the spirit of this prayer, which all the buddhas of the past have prayed:

> *By the power and the truth of this practice:*
> *May all beings have happiness, and the causes of*
> *   happiness;*
> *May all be free from sorrow, and the causes of sorrow;*
> *May all never be separated from the sacred happiness*
> *   which is sorrowless;*
> *And may all live in equanimity, without too much*
> *   attachment and too much aversion,*
> *And live believing in the equality of all that lives.*

December 16

I often think of the great masters and imagine beings who have their depth of realization as magnificent mountain eagles, who soar above both life and death and see them for what they are, in all their mysterious, intricate interrelation.

To see through the eyes of the mountain eagle, the view of realization, is to look down on a landscape in which the boundaries that we imagined existed between life and death shade into each other and dissolve. The physicist David Bohm has described reality as being "unbroken wholeness in flowing movement."

What is seen by the masters, then, seen directly and with total understanding, is that flowing movement and that unbroken wholeness. What we, in our ignorance, call "life" and what we, in our ignorance, call "death" are merely different aspects of that wholeness and that movement.

December 17

When you have learned, through discipline, to simplify your life, and so practiced the mindfulness of
meditation, and through it loosened the hold of aggression, clinging, and negativity on your whole being, the
wisdom of insight can slowly dawn. And in the all-
revealing clarity of its sunlight, this insight can show
you, distinctly and directly, both the subtlest workings
of your own mind and the nature of reality.

December 18

One great master in the nineteenth century had a disciple who was very thick-headed. The master had taught him again and again, trying to introduce him to the nature of his mind. Still he did not get it. Finally, the master became furious and told him: "Look, I want you to carry this bag full of barley up to the top of that mountain over there. But you mustn't stop and rest. Just keep on going until you reach the top."

The disciple was a simple man, but he had unshakable devotion and trust in his master, and he did exactly as he had been told. The bag was heavy and it took him a long time.

At last, when he reached the top, he dropped the bag. He slumped to the ground, overcome with exhaustion, but deeply relaxed. All his resistance had dissolved, and with it his ordinary mind. At that instant, he suddenly realized the nature of his mind. He ran back down the mountain, and, against all convention, burst into his master's room.

"I think I've got it now . . . I've really got it!"

His master smiled at him knowingly. "So you had an interesting climb up the mountain, did you?"

December 19

The practice of mindfulness, of bringing the scattered mind home, and so of bringing the different aspects of our being into focus, is called Peacefully Remaining or Calm Abiding.

All the fragmented aspects of ourselves, which had been at war, settle and dissolve and become friends. In that settling we begin to understand ourselves more, and sometimes even have glimpses of the radiance of our fundamental nature.

December 20

Remaining in the clarity and confidence of Rigpa allows all your thoughts and emotions to liberate naturally and effortlessly within its vast expanse, like writing in water, or painting in the sky. If you truly perfect this practice, karma has no chance to be accumulated, and in this state of aimless, carefree abandon, what Dudjom Rinpoche calls "uninhibited, naked ease," the karmic law of cause and effect can no longer bind you in any way.

To learn how to die is to learn how to live; to learn how to live is to learn how to act not only in this life but in the lives to come. To transform yourself truly and learn how to be reborn as a transformed being to help others is really to help the world in the most powerful way of all.

Let us dare to imagine now what it would be like to live in a world where a significant number of people took the opportunity, offered by the teachings, to devote part of their lives to serious spiritual practice, to recognize the nature of their minds, and so to use the opportunity of their deaths to move closer to buddhahood, and to be reborn with one aim, that of serving and benefiting others.

December 22

How can the wisdom mind of the buddhas be introduced? Imagine the nature of mind as your face; it is always with you, but you cannot see it without help. Now imagine that you have never seen a mirror before. The introduction by the master is like holding up a mirror suddenly in which you can, for the first time, see your face reflected.

Just like your face, this pure awareness of Rigpa is not something "new" that the master is giving you that you did not have before, nor is it something you could possibly find outside of yourself. It has always been yours, and has always been with you, but up until that startling moment you have never actually seen it directly.

December 23

In the West, people tend to be absorbed by what I call "the technology of meditation." The modern world, after all, is fascinated by mechanisms and machines and addicted to purely practical formulas. But by far the most important feature of meditation is not the technique but the spirit: the skillful, inspired and creative way in which we practice, which could also be called "the posture."

The masters say: *"If you create an auspicious condition in your body and your environment, then meditation and realization will automatically arise."* Talk about posture is not esoteric pedantry; the whole point of assuming a correct posture is to create a more inspiring environment for meditation, for the awakening of Rigpa.

There is a connection between the posture of the body and the mind. Mind and body are interrelated, and meditation arises naturally once your posture and attitude are inspired.

December 24

Mipham, a great Tibetan master who lived around the late 1900s, was a kind of Himalayan Leonardo da Vinci. He is said to have invented a clock, a cannon, and an airplane. But once each of them was complete, he destroyed it, saying it would only be the cause of further distraction.

December 25

For as long as space exists
And sentient beings endure,
May I too remain,
To dispel the misery of the world.

SHANTIDEVA

December 26

Compassion is a far greater and nobler thing than pity. Pity has its roots in fear and carries a sense of arrogance and condescension, sometimes even a smug feeling of "I'm glad it's not me." As Stephen Levine says: "When your fear touches someone's pain it becomes pity; when your love touches someone's pain, it becomes compassion." To train in compassion is to know that all beings are the same and suffer in similar ways, to honor all those who suffer, and to know that you are neither separate from nor superior to anyone.

Just as the ocean has waves, and the sun has rays, so the mind's own radiance is its thoughts and emotions. The ocean has waves, yet the ocean is not particularly disturbed by them. The waves are the *very nature* of the ocean. Waves will rise, but *where* do they go? Back into the ocean. And where do the waves come from? The ocean.

In the same manner, thoughts and emotions are the radiance and expression of the *very nature* of the mind. They rise from the mind, but where do they dissolve? Back into the mind. Whatever rises, do not see it as a particular problem. If you do not impulsively react, if you are only patient, it will once again settle into its essential nature.

When you have this understanding, then rising thoughts only enhance your practice. But when you do not understand what they intrinsically are—the radiance of the nature of your mind—then your thoughts become the seed of confusion. So have a spacious, open, and compassionate attitude toward your thoughts and emotions, because in fact your thoughts are your family, the family of your mind. Before them, as Dudjom Rinpoche used to say: "Be like an old wise man, watching a child play."

It is crucial now that an enlightened vision of death and dying should be introduced throughout the world at all levels of education. Children should not be "protected" from death, but introduced, while young, to the true nature of death and what they can learn from it.

Why not introduce this vision, in its simplest forms, to all age groups? Knowledge about death, about how to help the dying, and about the spiritual nature of death and dying should be made available to all levels of society; it should be taught, in depth and with real imagination, in schools and colleges and universities of all kinds; and especially and most important, it should be available in teaching hospitals to nurses and doctors who will look after the dying and who have so much responsibility to them.

December 29

Where exactly is our buddha nature? It is in the sky-like nature of our mind. Utterly open, free and limitless, it is fundamentally so simple and so natural that it can never be complicated, corrupted, or stained, so pure that it is beyond even the concept of purity and impurity.

To talk of this nature of mind as skylike is, of course, only a metaphor that helps us to begin to imagine its all-embracing boundlessness; for the buddha nature has a quality the sky cannot have, that of the radiant clarity of awareness.

It is said: "It is simply your flawless present awareness, cognizant and empty, naked and awake."

December 30

"Once you have the View, although the delusory perceptions of samsara may arise in your mind, you will be like the sky; when a rainbow appears in front of it, it's not particularly flattered, and when the clouds appear it's not particularly disappointed either. There is a deep sense of contentment. You chuckle from inside as you see the facade of samsara and nirvana; the View will keep you constantly amused, with a little inner smile bubbling away all the time."

DILGO KHYENTSE RINPOCHE

December 31

Men come and they go and they trot and they dance, and never a word about death. All well and good. Yet when death does come—to them, their wives, their children, their friends—catching them unawares and unprepared, then what storms of passion overwhelm them, what cries, what fury, what despair!. . .

To begin depriving death of its greatest advantage over us, let us adopt a way clean contrary to that common one; let us deprive death of its strangeness, let us frequent it, let us get used to it; let us have nothing more often in mind than death. . . . We do not know where death awaits us: so let us wait for it everywhere.

To practice death is to practice freedom. A man who has learned how to die has unlearned how to be a slave.

MONTAIGNE

MY TEACHERS

JAMYANG KHYENTSE CHÖKYI LODRÖ

DUDJOM RINPOCHE

Photo: Frederik Leboyer

DILGO KHYENTSE RINPOCHE
WITH SOGYAL RINPOCHE

Photo: Heiko Rah

NYOSHUL KHEN RINPOCHE

Photo: Philippe Lelluch

KHANDRO TSERING CHÖDRÖN

Photo: Mark Tracy

ABOUT THE AUTHOR

Sogyal Rinpoche was born in Tibet and raised as a son by one of the most revered spiritual teachers of the twentieth century, Jamyang Khyentse Chökyi Lodrö. From early childhood, he enjoyed a particularly warm and intimate relationship with this great master and was steeped in the atmosphere of wisdom, compassion, and devotion that surrounded him. This instilled in Rinpoche a deep understanding of the heart essence of the Buddhist teachings, one that grew out of his own experience, and that, when combined with his traditional training as an incarnate Lama, was to prepare him for his future role as a teacher.

After Jamyang Khyentse passed away, Sogyal Rinpoche continued to study with his two other principal masters, Dudjom Rinpoche and Dilgo Khyentse Rinpoche, who were the main inspiration behind the work in the West. In 1971 he went to England, where he studied Comparative Religion at Cambridge University. He began to teach in 1974 and has since been in increasing demand, teaching continuously in western and eastern Europe, the United States, Australia, and the East.

Rinpoche sees his life's work as that of transplanting the teachings of Buddha to the West by offering a training in the vision set out in *The Tibetan Book of Living and Dying*. This training can enable people who follow it to understand, embody, and integrate the teachings in their everyday lives and so be of the greatest possible benefit to others and to the world. Few teachers have Rinpoche's gift for communication, and living and teaching in the West now for more than twenty years has given him a profound insight into the western mind. He is known for the warmth, humor, and clarity with which he cuts through religious, cultural, and psychological barriers to reveal the heart of Buddha's vision. By sharing his personal experiences, with compelling examples drawn from everyday life, he is able to evoke a vivid feeling and flavor of the inner truth of the teachings by relating them directly to each student's own experience.

Sogyal Rinpoche embodies the dynamic energy, generosity of spirit, and directness of communication that are the hallmarks of the great Dzogchen tradition to which he belongs.

RIGPA

Sogyal Rinpoche has given the name Rigpa to the unique network of centers and groups of students around the world who follow the teachings and practice of Dzogchen under his guidance. Their vision, and their aim, is to make the Buddhist teachings available to as many people as possible, across all possible barriers of race, color, and creed, and to create supportive and inspiring environments to encourage their study and practice.

In various countries around the world, Rigpa has city centers that offer regular courses on meditation, compassion, and every other aspect of Buddhist wisdom for the modern world. Rigpa has played a major part in presenting to the West the most eminent Buddhist masters of all traditions, including His Holiness the Dalai Lama. In Rigpa's International Center in London, alongside the Buddhist teachings, different contemporary approaches are explored, from psychotherapy and healing, the arts and sciences, to the study of death and caring for the dying.

Central to Rigpa's program is the intensive training conducted by Sogyal Rinpoche during retreats of up to three months. They take place every year in Europe, the United States, and Australia. Rinpoche has founded retreat centers in the countryside in France and Ireland.

Rigpa also supports the work of many great masters in the East and sponsors the Dzogchen Monastery and its reconstruction in Kollegal, Mysore, southern India.

For details of Sogyal Rinpoche's teaching program
and courses at Rigpa, for information on anything
referred to in this book, for audio cassettes of Sogyal
Rinpoche's teachings, or for details on how to make an
offering for the dead, please contact the following:

United States
Santa Cruz
RIGPA
P.O. Box 607
Santa Cruz, CA 95061-0607
Tel: (1 408) 454–9103
Fax: (1 408) 454–0917

Britain
London
RIGPA
330 Caledonian Road
London N1 1BB
Tel: (44 71) 700–0185
Fax: (44 71) 609–6068

Germany
Berlin
RIGPA
Hasenheide 9
10967 Berlin
Tel: (49 30) 694–6433
Fax: 49 30) 694–65 83

France
Paris
RIGPA
22 rue Burq
75018 Paris
Tel: (33 1) 42–54–53–25
Fax: (33 1) 42–54–00–19

Montpellier
Lerab Ling Retreat Centre
L'Engayresque
34650 Roqueredonde
Tel: (33 67) 44–41–99
Fax: (33 67) 44–44–20

Switzerland
Zurich
RIGPA
P.O. Box 253
8059 Zurich

Netherlands
Amsterdam
Stichting RIGPA
Sint Agnietenstraat 22
1012 EG Amsterdam
Tel: (31 20) 623–8022

Ireland
Dublin
2nd Floor,
12 Wicklow Street
Dublin 2
Tel: (353 1) 540–480
Fax: (353 1) 540–480

Dzogchen Beara
Garranes
Allihies
Tel: (353 27) 730–32
Fax: (353 27) 731–77

Australia
Sydney
RIGPA
12/37 Nicholson Street
Balmain, NSW 2041
Tel: (61 2) 555–9952
Fax: (61 2) 973–2029